Handbook of Instructional Leadership

How Really Good Principals Promote Teaching and Learning

Jo Blase ▪ Joseph Blase

CORWIN PRESS, INC.
A Sage Publications Company
Thousand Oaks, California

For information:

Corwin Press, Inc.
A Sage Publications Company
2455 Teller Road
Thousand Oaks, California 91320
E-mail: order@corwin.sagepub.com

SAGE Publications Ltd.
6 Bonhill Street
London EC2A 4PU
United Kingdom

SAGE Publications India Pvt. Ltd.
M-32 Market
Greater Kailash I
New Delhi 110 048 India

Printed in the United States of America

Library of Congress Cataloging-in-Publication Data

Blase, Jo Roberts.
   Handbook of instructional leadership : How really good principals promote teaching and learning / Jo Blase, Joseph Blase.
      p.   cm.
   Includes bibliographical references.
   ISBN 0-8039-6553-2 (cloth : acid-free paper). — ISBN 0-8039-6554-0 (pbk. : acid-free paper)
      1. School supervision—United States—Handbooks, manuals, etc.
   2. Educational leadership—United States—Handbooks, manuals, etc.
   I. Blase, Joseph.   II. Title.
   LB2806.4.B63   1997
   371.2'03—dc21   97-45258

This book is printed on acid-free paper.

98 99 00 01 02 03 10 9 8 7 6 5 4 3 2

Production Editor: S. Marlene Head
Editorial Assistant: Kristen L. Gibson
Typesetter: Andrea D. Swanson
Cover Designer: Marcia M. Rosenburg

Contents

Foreword

During a break at a conference for educational leaders I attended recently, I was chatting with a colleague who taught a course on instructional leadership. One of her former graduate students, now a school principal, stopped to say hello. Within a few moments the conversation turned to the coursework the former student had taken during his graduate program: "I really enjoyed your course on instructional leadership," he said to my colleague, a professor with a reputation as an outstanding teacher. "I don't get much of a chance to use instructional leadership in the real world," he continued with a smile, "because I'm too busy with all of the day-to-day responsibilities of being a principal." My colleague's only response was nonverbal, somewhere between a smile and a grimace. As I listened to this conversation, I reflected on the fact that many school administrators had expressed the same notion to me; for these principals, instructional leadership, like solar energy, is an interesting concept but a low priority. They *wish* that they had more time to devote to it. But the "real world" of the principalship that they describe—a world of discipline referrals, parental complaints, and bureaucratic paperwork—leaves little room, they believe, for any instructional leadership beyond the traditional teacher evaluation process that they carry out once or twice a year. I have heard so many administrators state this belief that I refer to it as part of the "conventional wisdom" of traditional school principals.

In this book Blase and Blase prove that conventional wisdom concerning the principal and instructional leadership is utterly wrong.

Put positively, the research reported on the following pages proves convincingly that good principals are, first and foremost, good instructional leaders. Based on the comprehensive description of how instructional supervision is actually practiced and how it affects teachers, the Blases provide strong support for the general premise that "facilitative, supportive actions by principals as instructional leaders have powerful effects on classroom instruction," as well as the specific premise that "spoken language has a powerful impact on teachers' instructional behavior."

The Blases' research shows good instructional supervision to have such positive impacts on teaching and learning (and ineffective or nonexistent instructional supervision to have such negative impacts) that no one who reads this book will be able to justify the relegation of instructional leadership to the margins of educational administration. I have always believed that one reason many principals attend poorly or not at all to their instructional leadership responsibilities is that they lack information concerning exactly *how* one provides effective instructional supervision. The Blases' detailed descriptions of the behaviors of good instructional leaders, contrasted with equally detailed descriptions of ineffective behaviors, provide the data-based knowledge that principals need to develop or enhance their own instructional supervision.

Whether describing the good principal's role in instructional conferences, staff development, and teacher reflection or the principal's use of visibility, praise, and autonomy, the authors provide data-based descriptions of the goals that principals have when they use particular instructional leadership strategies, specific examples of those strategies, and specific impacts the strategies have on teachers. For each area of instructional leadership addressed in the book, summaries of research results serve as the skeleton, and extensive quotes from teachers who participated in the study flesh out the research findings. Blase and Blase present us with a treasure trove of basic knowledge about instructional leadership (five instructional conference strategies, six ways principals support the study of teaching, six principal behaviors that foster teacher reflection, and so on), but their work goes beyond merely reporting strategies used by good instructional leaders. Their rich descriptions of principals' motives, behaviors, and impacts, combined with revealing quotes from teachers, bring to life for the reader such concepts as *inquiry, reflection, collaboration, empowerment,* and *learning community.* They enable the reader to encounter the spirit of schools where these ideas have become a reality. In the same vein, the authors' findings and teachers' quotes provide a distressing view of the negative impact on teachers from principals' failure to effectively facilitate instructional conferences, staff development, and teacher reflection; in such cases, interruption, abandonment, criticism, and authoritarian control abound. Indeed, the contrast of good and ineffective behaviors is so stark, so compelling that the reader is left with a sense of urgency, with a conviction that the findings reported here need to be disseminated as soon as possible to inservice and preservice principals, central office administrators, policymakers, and professors of educational administration!

Another feature of this book that I appreciate is the way that Blase and Blase integrate their research findings with existing literature from a variety of related areas of study including models of teaching, adult development, critical theory, organizational theory, the change process, and leadership theory. By emphasizing the *interaction and interdependence* of all of these areas with instructional leadership, the Blases are laying the foundations for a *comprehensive approach* to school reform, with instructional leadership as the integrative sine qua non of school improvement.

At the beginning of this foreword I told the story of the principal who didn't have much time for instructional leadership because he was too busy with "the day-to-day responsibilities of being a principal." If I see that principal again, I plan to recommend that he read this book. At the very least it will offer him a "real world" radically different from the real world in which he currently operates, a world in which instructional leadership is the principal's most important function, and in which *good* instructional leadership has an enormously positively impact on teachers and teaching. The research presented in this book just might change that principal's view of what the principalship is all about.

In closing, I believe it is important to point out to readers not yet familiar with the authors that this book represents the latest publication in an impressive, thematic *body of work* developed by the authors, sometimes writing together, sometimes as individual authors, and other times with other coauthors. The Blases' work has focused on the related topics of the work-lives of teachers, supervision, instructional leadership, micropolitics in schools, teacher empowerment, and shared school governance. This work, then, can be viewed as an important piece of a larger whole the authors have been developing for some time now. They are to be commended for both this exceptional book and their overall contribution to the field of educational leadership.

STEPHEN P. GORDON
Southwest Texas State University

Preface

This book is written for practicing and prospective instructional leaders—including principals, assistant principals, lead teachers, department chairpersons, curriculum directors, and staff developers—who want to develop reflective, collaborative, problem-solving contexts for dialogue about instruction. It is about what *really good* instructional leaders do to enhance teaching and learning and the effects that their behaviors have on teachers' performance and well-being.

Disagreement about the essential nature of instructional supervision has existed for well over 100 years. Indeed, the *practice* of instructional supervision has admittedly been plagued by images of control and bureaucratic snooping in classrooms. Power-oriented administrators wielding reductionist algorithms for good teaching have all too often prevailed in learning matters. Conversely, collegiality among educators, teacher empowerment, purposeful inquiry, and encouragement to reflect and experiment—the healthy counterpoints to common practice—too infrequently are found.

Interestingly, we noticed some congruence between the practices of empowering principals we studied in earlier projects and the practices of principals deemed to be effective instructional leaders. Those discoveries led us to mount a comprehensive study of principals' *instructional leadership behaviors* and *their effects on teachers*, the findings of which are reported herein.

We believe this book will illuminate basic elements of effective instructional leadership and describe specifically how it supports both teacher and student learning. Because these elements emerge only after critical review of the behaviors of good leaders and, even more important, study of the effects of those behaviors on teachers and their work, we have included many comments about effects from teachers.

The Handbook of Instructional Leadership: How Really Good Principals Promote Teaching and Learning is drawn from a study of more than 800 teachers from public elementary, middle, and high schools in several regions of the United States. We asked these teachers to describe in detail the characteristics (e.g., strategies, behaviors, attitudes, and goals) of instructional supervisors (i.e., school principals) that influence, positively and negatively, their classroom instruction. We also asked them to discuss the personal and professional effects of related principal-teacher interactions. Thus, this book is representative of teachers' perspectives, and those perspectives were reported within a protocol that encouraged free expression and inclusion of details.

Specifically, we present descriptions of what good principals actually do that leads to such impacts as improved teacher morale and motivation, enhanced self-esteem and confidence, and reflectively oriented instructional behavior. We also present relevant concepts, models, and strategies from the literature that will help practitioners think through their approach to instructional leadership. Taken together, our database and the literature advocate a powerful holistic model of instructional leadership based on collaboration, reflection, and inquiry.

What does good instructional leadership look like? Which approaches to instructional leadership enhance or hinder teaching and learning? Chapter 1 presents a brief overview of the professional literature on instructional leadership and supervision as well as a brief description of the study on which this book is based. Chapters 2, 3, and 4 focus, respectively, on three fundamental themes of instructional leadership—talking with teachers, promoting teachers' professional growth, and fostering teacher reflection. In reading these chapters, practitioners will see how specific principal behaviors help to build a culture of collaboration, equality, and lifelong study of teaching and learning. In Chapters 5, 6, and 7 we discuss principals' use of visibility, praise, and autonomy—as juxtaposed with abandonment, criticism, and control—and their effects on teachers. Chapter 8, the final chapter, summarizes our findings and conclusions, presents our view of good instructional leadership, and offers suggestions for building school-based communities. Research methods are found in the Resource section.

This book describes not only what good instructional leaders are doing but also what can be expected when they support (as well as when they harm) teachers, teaching, and learning in our schools. Dramatic findings presented in the teachers' own words portray effective instructional leadership as an exciting, collaborative inquiry into the complex and perplexing world of teaching and learning; therein lies our hope of becoming a learning community.

Acknowledgments

We deeply appreciate the efforts of hundreds of teachers in completing the study on which this book is based. We also thank our colleagues in the university community for their wise counsel; our secretary, Donna Bell, for her patience and her flawless work; our students and practitioners, Marcia Davidson, Mary Hensien, Randall Richards, and Ellen Sabatini, for their critical review and commentary; and our editor, Cheryl Smith, for her perfection in expression.

Jo Blase
Joseph Blase

About the Authors

Jo Blase is Professor of Educational Leadership at the University of Georgia and a former public school teacher, principal, and director of staff development. She received a Ph.D. in educational administration, curriculum, and supervision in 1983 from the University of Colorado at Boulder. Through work with the Beginning Principal Study National Research Team, the Georgia League of Professional Schools, and public and private school educators with whom she consults throughout the United States, she has pursued her interest in preparation for and entry to educational and instructional leadership as it relates to supervisory discourse.

Winner of the 1997 University of Georgia College of Education Teacher Educator Award and the 1983 American Association of School Administrators Outstanding Research Award, Blase's recent publications include articles in the *Journal of Staff Development,* the *Journal of Curriculum and Supervision, Educational Administration Quarterly,* and *The Alberta Journal of Educational Research;* and three books, *Empowering Teachers: What Successful Principals Do* (with Joseph Blase, Corwin, 1994), *Democratic Principals in Action: Eight Pioneers* (with Joseph Blase, Gary Anderson, and Sherry Dungan, Corwin, 1995), and *The Fire Is Back: Principals Sharing School Governance* (with Joseph Blase, Corwin, 1997). She has authored chapters on becoming a principal, school renewal, supervision, and organizational development. She also conducts research on supervisory discourse among physicians as medical educators.

Joseph Blase is Professor of Educational Leadership at the University of Georgia. Since receiving his Ph.D. in 1980 from Syracuse University, his research has focused on understanding the work lives of teachers. He has published many studies in the areas of teacher stress, relationships between teachers' personal and professional lives, teacher socialization, and principal-teacher relationships. His work concentrating on school-level micropolitics received the 1988 Davis Memorial Award given by the University Council for Educational Administration.

Blase edited *The Politics of Life in Schools: Power, Conflict, and Cooperation* (winner of the 1994 Critic's Choice Award sponsored by the American Education Studies Association, Sage, 1991); coauthored, with Peggy Kirby, *Bringing Out the Best in Teachers* (Corwin, 1994); coauthored with Jo Blase, Gary Anderson, and Sherry Dungan, *Democratic Principals in Action: Eight Pioneers* (Corwin, 1995); coauthored with Gary Anderson, *The Micropolitics of Educational Leadership* (Teachers College Press, 1995); and coauthored with Jo Blase, *The Fire Is Back: Principals Sharing School Governance* (Corwin, 1997). His numerous articles appear in journals such as the *American Education Research Journal* and *Educational Administration Quarterly*.

Dedication

It is our pleasure, indeed our privilege, to dedicate this book to our dear friend and colleague, Dr. Art Blumberg. Throughout his career, Art has been a champion of children and educators alike, a model for scholars, and a personal hero to us. Indeed, findings of the research on which this book is based were foreshadowed in Art's own assertions that staff development is "work-oriented conversation," and "If I were a principal today, I would try to conceive my role primarily as an initiator of conversations about teaching with my faculty."

Recently, when asked for his thoughts on the past, present, and future of instructional leadership and supervision, Art shared what follows:

As I reflect on the practice of supervision as I have come to understand it, my inclination is to see the supervisory system as relatively *ineffectual.* As I say this, I do not mean to imply that there have not been many, many times when an individual supervisor has been fantastically successful with regard to a single teacher. Nor do I mean that there have not been a large number of school principals who have created schools in which the teachers (and the principal) deliberately try to understand the classroom as a *learning system* and adjust their behavior to the demands of the system. I do not, however, think this is the *norm* of the system, and it is the norm with which I am concerned.

What I think the future is entitled to is a view of school supervision as an instructional system for the adults in a school whose primary role is to help kids learn. I think the school in which the teachers, counselors, and principal join in an ongoing conversation about *teaching as an exquisitely complicated craft* is what is required. And I mean *conversation* literally. Such a perspective naturally includes treating those adults as people who are interested in and have a stake in their work.

We thank Art for his wonderful contributions to conversations with us, and we hope our work, like his, sparks many more conversations among educators about the nature of good instructional leadership.

PART I

The Art and Science of Instructional Leadership

The Craft of Teacher Supervision

The principal of a successful school is not the instructional leader but the coordinator of teachers as instructional leaders.

Glickman, 1991, p. 7

During the past few years, many school districts have, in varying degrees, decentralized operations to implement forms of school-based shared decision making in their efforts to restructure schools. Hand in hand with such efforts has been a nascent move to empower and professionalize teachers, notably in the areas of instructional supervision and staff development. In addition, "supervision," as the external imposition of bureaucratic, rational authority, has been challenged by many who work to professionalize teaching.

As a result, many of today's successful schools are fast becoming centers of shared inquiry and decision making; teachers are moving toward a collective—not an individual—practice of teaching. They are collaborating with each other and with supervisors in a "kind of mutual nudging in the profoundly cooperative search for answers" to instructional problems (Dowling & Sheppard, 1976, p. 5). Instructional leadership is being shared with teachers, and in its best forms it is being cast as coaching, reflection, collegial investigation, study teams, explorations into uncertain matters, and problem solving.

3

Alternatives, not directives or criticism, are the focus, and administrators and teachers work together as a "community of learners" engaged in professional and moral (even noble) service to students.

In this age of democratization, when bureaucratic authority is being dismantled, we must examine the notion of collaboration as it relates to the practice of leadership and, in particular, to instructional supervision. *Clearly, there is a compelling need for practicing and aspiring administrators and supervisors to search for ways to encourage collegiality and to significantly improve instructional supervision in today's changing schools.*

Unfortunately, there are no published comprehensive descriptions of how instructional supervision is actually practiced in schools and how teachers are affected by such supervision. What exists are exploratory studies of the supervisory conference (Roberts, 1991a), research on the micropolitics of supervisor-teacher talk in public schools (e.g., Blase & Blase, 1996), as well as related studies of precepting in medical schools (Blase & Hekelman, 1996; Hekelman & Blase, 1996). Moreover, such studies of supervision have generated only scant data-based descriptions of the critical aspects of the supervisor's role in implementing the supervision process (Holland, 1989; Short, 1995).

Our Study

Which characteristics (e.g., strategies, behaviors, attitudes, and goals) of school principals[1] influence, positively and negatively, teachers' classroom instruction? What is it about supervisor-teacher interaction—with a specific emphasis on the talk that occurs in instructional supervisory conferences—that enables teachers to learn and apply such learnings to classroom instruction? Our study of both positive and negative principal behaviors with regard to instruction—the basis of this book—sheds light on these and other critical questions so far unaddressed by empirical research.

In addition to offering many clues about the various paths to successful instructional supervision, we also *describe the benefits of developing reflective, collaborative, problem-solving contexts for dialogue about instruction.* Along these lines, we examine and describe a specialized form of teacher thinking—reflection—that arises from a teacher's questions about perplexing classroom experiences and that leads to purposeful inquiry and problem resolution (Dewey, 1933). Indeed, we confirm that in effective principal-teacher interaction about instruction, processes such as inquiry, reflection, exploration, and experimentation prevail; teachers build repertoires of flexible alternatives rather than collecting rigid teaching procedures and methods (Schön, 1987).

The study we describe in this book was based on two broad premises: (1) Spoken language has a powerful impact on teachers' instructional behavior and (2) facilitative, supportive actions by principals as instructional leaders have powerful effects on classroom instruction. These premises are derived from Hymes's notion of "conversational competence" (1971), which posits that by studying interaction (with specific emphasis on communicative competence), we can better understand instructional interactions (such as those between principals and teachers) and conference dialogue in varied contexts. Indeed, as the context of supervision shifts from oversight and evaluation to collaboration and reflection (Glickman, Gordon, & Ross-Gordon, 1995), the elements of such understandings can be applied to discussions among peer teachers, coaches, and mentors.

Our Study Sample

Hymes (1982) contends that the study of activity occurring in various contexts is useful for demystifying and explicating experiences such as instructional supervision and, in particular, the dialogue that occurs between instructional supervisors (e.g., a principal, another administrator, or a lead teacher) and teachers. We agree; our study has yielded new knowledge about the supervisor-teacher relationship that goes well beyond the solid but singular research of three decades ago. We did this by closely examining teachers' reports of instructionally oriented situations as they naturally occurred in a variety of school settings, an approach that has been recommended by researchers and theorists in the field for some time, but seldom used (Blumberg, 1980).

Data for this book was collected from more than 800 teachers working in public elementary, middle, and high schools in the Southeastern, Midwestern, and Northwestern United States. Teachers completed open-ended questionnaires on which they wrote detailed descriptions of principals' positive and negative characteristics and exactly how such characteristics affected them and their performance in the classroom. (See Resource for a more complete discussion.)

Research Question

The primary question driving our study was, What positive and negative characteristics of school principals (e.g., strategies, behaviors, attitudes, goals) and principal-teacher interactions (e.g., informal conversations, discussions centered on instructional matters, discussion regarding requests for assistance or materials, discussions about formal or informal procedures and policies) influence (positively or adversely) teachers' classroom instruction? We wanted to illuminate the following:

- What are teachers' perceptions of principals' characteristics that influence their instructional work?
- What are the effects of these perceptions on teachers' instructional performance?
- Are collaborative characteristics such as mutual respect, tolerance, acceptance, commitment, courage, sharing, and teaming in evidence in interaction between principal-supervisors and teachers?
- Are the essential aspects of supervisory practice that enhance teaching/learning (e.g., reflective conversations, the implementation of improvement plans within individual classrooms) addressed or neglected in formal or informal conferences?
- What must principals learn in order to have instructional and, in particular, communicative competence?
- What are the logic, etiquette, and social and cultural values associated with successful instructional conferences?
- How do our findings compare with the findings of recent studies focusing on topics like teacher control and principal and teacher conceptual levels (Grimmett, 1984)?

In this book we examine the extant research on instructional supervisory behavior and its effects and consider the developmental aspects of instructional supervisory practice. Our findings about principals' speech and behaviors capture the diversity and complexity of supervisory acts—a topic of study commonly ignored by researchers. Most certainly, this book is the first in-depth, empirical report of the actual experiences of teachers in instructionally oriented interactions (cf. Herbert & Tankersley, 1993). As such, it explores in detail teachers' perspectives on principals' instructionally oriented behaviors and interactions and their impacts on a range of dimensions of classroom instruction.

From our study, we conclude, among other things, that even good instructional leaders, that is, those who primarily had positive goals and attitudes and used positive strategies, often met with only mixed success in their attempts to initiate and sustain a robust reflective orientation in teachers regarding both their day-to-day teaching and professional growth. Others have suggested that this is partly because principals often lack requisite communication skills (Pugach & Johnson, 1990) and the knowledge essential for planning, change, and instructional improvement (e.g., facilitation, direct observation, conferring, staff development, modeling, and teaching/learning). This volume illuminates some of these relevant issues.

The Instructional Supervision Legacy: From Control to Collaboration

In 1993, Cogan, Anderson, and Krajewski classified supervision approaches that have appeared in the professional literature between 1850 and 1990:

1. Scientific management
2. Democratic interaction approach
3. Cooperative supervision
4. Supervision as curriculum development
5. Clinical supervision
6. Group dynamics and peer emphasis
7. Coaching and instructional supervision

Krajewski (1996) describes contemporary approaches as *almost collaborative*; almost—not truly—collaborative, the author suggests, because power differentials still exist between principals and teachers, given the principals' evaluation responsibilities (power to judge) and change-agent role. Krajewski predicts that by the year 2015 supervision will consist of *structured options* (i.e., based on some standards and expectations, but also based on teachers' individual needs and goals, much like a student's Individualized Education Plan, or IEP).

However, the array of approaches to supervision noted above indicates that substantial disagreement about its essential nature has existed for more than 140 years. The *practice* of supervision is another matter. Despite the fact that many approaches to supervision are collaborative in nature, the practice of supervision has often been one of inspection, oversight, and judgment. Glanz (1995) concluded that today's supervision is nothing better than a "bureaucratic legacy of fault finding, inspectional supervision" and used terms like *snoopervision, protective political behavior,* and *a private cold war* (p. 107) to characterize the field. Sergiovanni (1992) referred to supervision as a "nonevent—a ritual they [supervisors and teachers] participate in according to well-established scripts without much consequence" (p. 203). More recently, Gordon (1997) stated, "In the present, control supervision [not collegiality and empowerment] still dominates professional practice" (p. 117).

We believe that although the idea of collegial supervision, in various forms, has existed for most of this century, advanced forms of collegiality are rarely found in practice. Indeed, democratic, cooperative, clinical, human resource–based, developmental, and transformational supervision, among others, have been widely advocated (Gordon, 1997) based on the principles of equality (not hierarchy), reflection, and growth (not compliance). For instance, Pajak (1993) noted that the goal (and, at times, the *emerging* practice) of supervision focuses on "helping teachers discover and construct professional knowledge and skills," in contrast with the established practice of "reinforcing specific prescribed teacher behavior and skills" (p. 318). He also noted that in much contemporary thinking, learning is viewed as contextual and complex, teaching is based on reflective judgment, and schools are seen as democratic teaching and learning communities.

Likewise, Schön's (1988) definition of instructional supervision emphasizes collegial supervision and specifically focuses on support, guidance, and encouragement of *reflective teaching*; and Glickman (1992) described ideal supervision as a *collaborative* endeavor enacted in a supportive environment that leads to an all-school action plan. To promote collegial forms of supervision, McBride and Skau (1995) have proposed that practitioners develop a *supervisory platform*—a combination of supervisory beliefs and educational philosophy—that includes building *trust, empowering* teachers, and fostering *reflection.*

They note, "The process of reflection, undertaken in an environment based on trust and seeking the empowerment of participants, constitutes a powerful potential for improved [supervisory and teaching] practice" (p. 277).

Relatedly, Reitzug and Cross (1993) have discussed an *inquiry-oriented* practice of supervision (i.e., "critical collaboration") that encourages teacher voice and acknowledges the contextuality and complexity of teaching. Here, the principal's role is one of facilitating a teacher's thinking about practice. More broadly, Smyth (1997) has suggested that supervision advance a discursive, collaborative, and critical study of the *micropolitics of the classroom* interaction; relinquish its technocratic surveillance of teachers; and work toward a just and democratic world. He recommends giving teachers more, rather than less, control over their teaching.

Research on Instructional Supervision

"A Review of Studies in the First 10 Volumes of the *Journal of Curriculum and Supervision*" (Short, 1995) indicated that only 82 articles in the area of supervision have been published. These articles addressed conceptions of supervision, supervision theory, legal issues in supervision, the work of supervisors in various roles, evaluation of supervisory practices, the supervisory conference, Schön's reflective practice, reflective practice and supervision, supervisory history, supervision research (inquiry approaches), and supervision research (areas requiring inquiry) (p. 88). In spite of the periodical's considerable contribution to the field, Short concludes that the *Journal of Curriculum and Supervision*—the primary source of published scholarly work in supervision in North America—has featured a dearth of research on supervision. Several authors have made the case for more research into the effects of supervision on teacher behavior, how supervision relates to teaching, supervisor characteristics, and conditions necessary for effective supervision.

Administration and supervision textbooks have been no more successful than the *Journal of Curriculum and Supervision* with regard to the quality and quantity of materials and research that they include. In fact, Glanz (1995) found that few administration textbooks address the area of supervision at all. One exception is Sergiovanni and

Starratt's (1993) text, wherein supervision is seen as a moral enterprise in which teachers work together as colleagues—using peer supervision, mentoring, and action research—to better understand practice.

By examining writings on both *supervision* (a subset of instructional leadership) and *instructional leadership*, we will see the *connections* between the actions a principal takes and the professional growth of teachers, teacher commitment, involvement, and innovativeness, on one hand, and increases in student learning, on the other hand. Observe below, for example, that the writers we cite consistently emphasize teachers' *professional growth* in their descriptions of supervision.

Regarding Supervision

Glickman (1985) defined the five tasks of supervision that have direct impact on instructional improvement as direct assistance, group development, staff development, curriculum development, and action research. The integration of these tasks, Glickman says, unites teachers' needs with the school's goals.

In research with a team of doctoral students at the University of Georgia, Pajak (1989) defined supervision in practice as follows (listed in order of importance as ranked by practitioners):

1. Communication
2. Staff development (professional growth)
3. Instructional program (improvement)
4. Planning and change (collaborative work)
5. Motivating and organizing (shared vision)
6. Observation and conferencing
7. Curriculum
8. Problem solving and decision making
9. Service to teachers (support for teaching and learning)
10. Personal development (reflection on beliefs, abilities, actions)
11. Community relations
12. Research and program evaluation (assessing outcomes and encouraging experimentation; Pajak, 1989, p. 73)

Taken together, Glickman and Pajak's descriptions of supervision succinctly conceptualize and illuminate the responsibilities and activities of what we broadly refer to as instructional leadership.

Regarding Instructional Leadership

Although school principals have long believed that instructional leadership (often conceived of as a blend of supervision, staff development, and curriculum development) facilitates school improvement (Smith & Andrews, 1989), until recently little knowledge of what behaviors comprise *good* instructional leadership has been available in the literature. Sheppard (1996) synthesized the research on instructional leadership behaviors, especially those linked to student achievement outcomes and, in contrast to most research, used a broad perspective of instructional leadership defined as interactions between leaders and followers wherein *the followers' beliefs and perceptions are viewed as important* (Hallinger & Murphy, 1987). Sheppard's findings contradict those of others who found that routine instructional leadership behaviors often negatively affect teachers, increase teacher docility, and reduce teacher innovation and creativity. Sheppard confirmed a *positive* and strong relationship between effective instructional leadership behaviors exhibited by principals and *teacher commitment, professional involvement*, and *innovativeness*. Principal behaviors connected to teachers' professional growth and performance were as follows:

- Framing school goals[+]
- Communicating school goals
- Supervising and evaluating instruction
- Coordinating the curriculum
- Monitoring student progress
- Protecting instructional time
- Maintaining high visibility[*]
- Providing incentives for teachers
- Promoting professional development[+*]
- Providing incentives for learning
  Key: * = Most influential behaviors, elementary school; + = most
  influential behaviors, high school (Sheppard, 1996, pp. 327, 339)

Specifically, Sheppard learned that *promoting teachers' professional development* was the most influential instructional leadership behavior at both the elementary and high school levels and that only three to five principal behaviors accounted for most of the influence on teachers' commitment, involvement, and innovativeness. (This suggests that principals who emphasize even a small number of critical instructional leadership behaviors can expect good results with teachers.) As might be expected, Sheppard explained that a school's unique context inevitably influences the effectiveness of the model of instructional leadership employed.

Other research highlights the importance of principals' instructional leadership to teachers' responses. For example, Leithwood (1994) linked principals' transformational instructional leadership to improvement in teachers' classroom behaviors, attitudes, and effectiveness. Unfortunately though, even transformational principals and teachers have great difficulty achieving true vision sharing and the deep commitment to improvement necessary to enhance student learning (Sergiovanni, 1995). Blase (1993) wrote, "The critical process of dynamic, open, and democratic interaction between leaders and others . . . is noticeably absent, and the decisional authority and responsibility of others are limited significantly" (p. 159).

Thus, although there exists an emerging knowledge base about the behaviors and potential of instructional leadership, the extant literature provides few clues on how principals and teachers together can achieve shared vision and commitment—a foundation necessary for school improvement.

Teacher Empowerment Related to Supervision and Instructional Leadership

Some researchers have studied the relationship between instructional leadership and teacher empowerment. To illustrate, from an intensive case study of instructional leadership, Reitzug (1994) constructed a taxonomy of empowering principal behavior that includes the following:

- **Support:** Creating a supportive environment for critique of instruction by educators
- **Facilitation:** Stimulating critique of instruction by educators
- **Possibility:** Making it possible to give educators voice by publishing and acting on results of critique

Reitzug's study was based on Prawat's (1991) framework for epistemological and political empowerment, which consists of two categories—"conversations with self" and "conversations with settings" (p. 738)—wherein teachers develop inquiry skills, critical reflection skills, and even sociopolitical insights through internal dialogue. Prawat argued that nurturing alternative modes of professional interaction is *key* to empowerment and instructional improvement. Reitzug demonstrated this; he found that principal behavior consisting of providing staff development, modeling inquiry, asking questions, encouraging risk taking, requiring justification of practices, and critique-by-wandering-around led to greater levels of teacher empowerment in the classroom. These *instructional leadership* behaviors are similar to those we found in research focusing on the practices of empowering instructional principals (Blase & Blase, 1994; Blase, Blase, Anderson, & Dungan, 1995; Blase & Blase, 1997).

School Reform Related to Instructional Supervision and Leadership

In addition to establishing clear connections between instructional leadership and teacher performance, research has also linked instructional leadership to efforts to improve schools. In a recent report to the educational community, Clark and Clark (1996) indicated that three instructional leadership processes undergirded six contemporary reform initiatives, including Foxfire, Accelerated Schools, The League of Professional Schools, Impact II, The Coalition of Essential Schools, and the Center for Educational Renewal. These leadership processes are (1) defining and sustaining educational purpose, (2) developing and nurturing community, and (3) fostering personal and organizational growth (Murphy, 1995, p. 2). Clark and Clark (1996) also stated that leadership processes, such as those listed below, emphasized the centrality of instruction and learning, as well as professional development:

- A strong sense of mission
- Shared vision
- Webs of communication
- Breakdown of hierarchies
- Shared governance

- Personal development
- Lifelong learning
- Learning communities

Current Issues in the Field

Glanz and Neville (1997) brought together writers in the field of supervision to debate the following controversial critical issues:

- Abolishing supervision
- Putting the S (supervision) back in ASCD (the Association for Supervision and Curriculum Development)
- The benefits of supervision to teachers
- Reconciling the estrangement between curriculum and supervision
- Coaching
- The name *supervision* itself
- Collegiality between supervisors and teachers
- The relationship between staff development and supervision
- National standards for preparation of supervisors
- The influence of business management practices
- The viability of clinical supervision
- How technology influences supervision

In their book, Glanz and Neville describe the lively debate that occurred; this description is followed by perspective papers dealing with moving to a *community* theory of supervision, supervision as *more than surveillance*, new supervisory *roles* in an age of complexity, the effects of *law* on supervision, and the *moral imperative* in advocating for *diversity*.

Glanz and Neville (1997) present dramatic evidence showing that although the field of supervision is in a state of flux, most scholars agree that (1) schools should be learning environments for all students and educators, and (2) the facilitation of learning and growth should be the *number one responsibility* of an educational leader.

Our book is about good principal leadership and how it supports teacher and student learning. This has been called supervision, instructional or educational leadership, or administration. (See Figure 1.1 for further discussion of the designation.) The book is also about what good principals do to facilitate empowerment and reform in schools. In the following chapters we present the findings from our study and discuss them in the context of relevant theory and research. In Chapters 2, 3, and 4, principal characteristics and their impacts on teachers in the areas of conferencing, staff development, and reflection are examined (i.e., Talking, Growing, and Reflecting—the TiGeR model; see Figure 1.2 for an overview of these three themes of instructional leadership, as we conceive it). In Part II we discuss additional findings related to principals' use of visibility, praise, and autonomy—juxtaposed with the negative behaviors of abandonment, criticism, and control. (See Figure 1.3 for an overview of these dichotomous behaviors and their effects on teachers.) In the final chapter we offer our view, based on all we have learned, of the status and future of instructional supervision.

Note

1. Although in many cases instructional supervisors are, in fact, school principals, they may also be lead teachers, department chairpersons, curriculum directors, and staff developers.

Words are powerful, and the term *supervision* could probably stand a change. But it is about much more than the name! We've all had this conversation before. Supervision smacks of something from the Dark Ages, a barbaric act of policing those who are only lately being acknowledged as professionals. And although we all recognize the need for "quality control" and even aggressive action on the part of a supervisor when incompetence in teaching our children is concerned, we also know that the hue and cry for the professionalization of teaching rings true. Even so, we cannot pretend that supervisors, given their institutionally vested authority to assess, are perceived as the equals of teachers, although we obviously need to redress the balance-of-power issue in supervision-teacher relationships. In fact, we may not yet understand all the complexities and exigencies of this supervision issue, but one thing is certain: The current state of affairs is like Dowling and Sheppard's (1976, p. 4) "low-grade fever," and we must minimize the tension and maximize the benefits of supervision.

So how do we do this? It is a thorny question. Although many of us consistently argue that talented, sincere supervisors who are also responsible for teacher evaluation can engage teachers in meaningful discussions about teaching and learning—and should do this in a nonthreatening way—we need to capture alternative ways to help teachers reflect critically on their actions, clarify their thinking, make explicit their theories-in-action, engage in critical analysis of self, and genuinely share.

Some supervisors are already doing this. Simple, traditional supervision is giving way to a new order, one that implies much more than just a new name (facilitation? collegial or peer observation? inclusive supervision?). Supervision as snoopervision or as rigid demands for conformity is the antithesis of shared inquiry and decision making. Today's supervision is position-free; it is supervision wherein leaders, teachers, and learners are all one and in which the underlying spirit is one of expansion of skills and spirit.

It seems we could at least give this new process a different, and more fitting, name. May I suggest that it is about collaboration, being one among equals, and having power with—not over—others? Perhaps Goldsberry's (1980) term, *colleague consultation*, comes close; in any event, Glickman (1992) said it well:

If "instructional leadership" were substituted [for supervision] . . . little meaning would be lost and much might be gained. To be blunt: as a field, we may no longer need the old words and connotations. Instead, we might be seeing every talented educator (regardless of role) as an instructional leader and supervisor of instruction. If so, indeed, the old order will have crumbled. (p. 3)

At the same time, Glanz (1997a) asserts that teachers certainly *want* informed, practical supervision. He suggests that the field need not be "politically correct by eschewing the [supervision] label . . . [because] working face-to-face with classroom teachers to refine teaching practice . . . is still supervision to me" (p. 129).

Figure 1.1. Supervision: Time for a Name Change?

An earlier version of this discussion appeared in J. R. Blase (1995).

Chapter 2	*Talk With Teachers* • Build trust. • Develop the group. • Foster collaboration and collegiality. • Support peer coaching. • Observe in classrooms. • Confer with teachers about teaching and learning. • Empower teachers. • Maintain visibility.
Chapter 3	*Promote Teachers' Professional Growth* • Study literature and proven programs. • Support practice of new skills, risk taking, innovation, and creativity. • Provide effective staff development programs. • Apply principles of adult growth and development. • Praise, support, and facilitate teachers' work. • Provide resources and time. • Give feedback and suggestions.
Chapter 4	*Foster Teacher Reflection* • Develop teachers' reflection skills in order to construct professional knowledge and develop sociopolitical insights. • Model and develop teachers' critical study (action research) skills. • Become inquiry oriented. • Use data to question, evaluate, and critique teaching and learning. • Extend autonomy to teachers.

Figure 1.2. Overview of Part I, Chapters 2, 3, 4: Three Themes of Instructional Leadership: Building a Culture of Collaboration, Equality, and Lifelong Study of Teaching and Learning Through Talk, Growth, and Reflection (the TiGeR Model)

Chapter 5	*Being Visible* results in: • High morale and motivation • Enhanced self-esteem • Increased sense of security • Reflection and reflectively oriented behavior	Vs.	*Interrupting and Abandoning* results in: • Anger • Low motivation • Psychic pain • Feelings of no support • Loss of respect for principal • Poor performance
Chapter 6	*Praising* results in: • High motivation • Feeling rewarded, cared about • Enhanced self-esteem and confidence • Willingness to comply • Reflection and reflectively oriented behavior	Vs.	*Criticizing* results in: • Anger • Low motivation • Damaged self-esteem • Fear • Confusion • Loss of respect and trust for principal • Appearing to comply; ignoring, avoiding principal • Resistance and rebellion • Cautiousness
Chapter 7	*Extending Autonomy* results in: • High motivation • Enhanced self-esteem and confidence • Increased sense of security and professional discretion • Reflection and reflectively oriented behavior	Vs.	*Maintaining Control* results in: • Limited involvement in decision making (false image of governance) • Sense of being manipulated • Feeling abused

Figure 1.3. Overview of Part II, Chapters 5, 6, 7: How Supervisors' Behaviors—Positive and Negative—Affect Teachers

The Conference:
Heart of Instructional Supervision

*Once mutual concerns and ideas are shared, and sugges-
tions are discussed, it [the conference] becomes a planning
conference in which teacher and supervisor, collaboratively, decide on continued use of effective, observable
teaching behaviors, further collection of observational data,
and/or work on a plan for the development of specific
teaching behaviors that enhance the teaching process.*

Ovando, 1991, p. 21

Our study indicates that principals who are good instructional
leaders develop a deep appreciation for the potential artistry of
an instructional conference with a teacher—that magical, creative,
intuitive, and reflective talk—as they discover the complexity and
challenge of conducting an effective conference. Principals struggle to
balance content with direction, human concerns with organizational
goals, the need for growth with the press of inertia, and formal
structure with creativity.

Such principals realize that most teachers expand their teaching
range only with *carefully designed support and assistance.* This is a
startling revelation for principals who had always assumed intuitively

that when given *minimal* information and assistance, most teachers would analyze their own teaching and formulate and act on growth plans in a self-directed and constructive manner.

Developing such understandings about teachers was intimidating and motivating: However, the principals described in our study seemed to capitalize on their drive to become good instructional supervisors by bolstering their skills in this lingering area of concern, the conference. We found that conducting a conference necessitated attainment of knowledge and mastery of a number of complex prerequisite skills and processes, including the following:

- Classroom observation and data-gathering methods
- Teaching methods, skills, and repertoires
- Understanding of the relationship between teaching and learning
- Data analysis
- Knowing how to make the conference reflective and nonthreatening
- Communication skills (e.g., acknowledging, paraphrasing, summarizing, clarifying, and elaborating on information)
- Awareness of the stage of development, career state, levels of abstraction and commitment, learning style, concerns about innovation, and background of the teacher

According to our data, attention to the knowledge and skill associated with such processes invariably helped principals gain confidence and operate on more sophisticated and complex levels in conferences, helped them provide support for teachers working toward instructional improvement, and helped principals make conferences more positive and growth-oriented for teachers. (As we shall see later, a principal's failure to attend to the conference has disastrous effects on teachers.)

Historically, approaches to supervisory practice have been grounded in a variety of paradigms such as positivism, phenomenology, and critical theory (May & Zimpher, 1986). The collaborative approach, first discussed by Cogan (1973) in his conception of clinical supervision (and supported by writers who used a blend of the aforementioned paradigms, such as Eisner [1982], Garman [1982], Glickman [1985], and Sergiovanni [1992]), challenged authoritarian, bureaucratic, traditional approaches to supervision. For instance, Garman (1982, 1990) criticized the "ritualistic" nature of the instructional conference and called for a transformation to genuineness and mutual problem solving. Others have reinforced Blumberg and Amidon's (1965) early research, which highlighted the importance of open-ended, collaborative, and nondirective behaviors in effective instructional conferences.

This chapter begins with a general description of the approaches and techniques used by successful principals with regard to instructional conferences with teachers. After a brief summary of the extant research on the instructional conference, a section on supervisor-teacher discourse discusses in detail the two primary strategies effective principals used in conferences described in our study—making suggestions and giving feedback—and their effects on teachers. Last, the principals' use of modeling, inquiry, and soliciting advice and opinions is discussed in brief sections.

Successful Approaches

Pajak (1993) recently described and compared the most popular and enduring approaches—classroom observation and conferencing (see Figure 2.1)—for improving classroom instruction. Both approaches are considered "clinical" because they consist of face-to-face interaction between teachers and supervisors. Figure 2.1 identifies a diverse group of four families of supervision—original clinical, humanistic/artistic, technical/didactic, and developmental/reflective models—each of which emphasizes different procedures for observation and feedback and different perspectives on the supervisor-teacher interaction in conferences.

Glickman's (1981, 1985) Developmental Supervision Model is one of the most practical and well-known; it represents the *approach* most frequently ascribed to (but at times not consistently adhered to) by the effective principals discussed in our study. This model includes the following:

- A *cycle* of preconference, observation, analysis and interpretation, postconference, and critique
- Consideration of a teacher's *levels* of abstraction, adult development, and concerns

1. Original clinical models
       Cogan (1973)
       Goldhammer (1969)
       Mosher & Purpel (1972)

2. Humanistic/artistic models
       Blumberg (1980)
       Eisner (1982)

3. Technical/didactic models
       Acheson & Gall (1997)
       Hunter (1979, 1987)
       Joyce & Showers (1995)

4. Developmental/reflective models
       Bowers & Flinders (1991)
       Costa & Garmston (1994)
       Garman (1982)
       Glickman, Gordon, & Ross-Gordon (1995)
       Retallick (1990)
       Schön (1983, 1987)
       Smyth (1990)
       Zeichner & Liston (1987)

Figure 2.1. Supervision Models Compared by Pajak (1993), With Primary References

- An *approach* ranging from nondirective to collaborative to directive (control and informational) behaviors on the part of the supervisor
- The opportunity for *peer supervision* among teachers

In practice, we found that many of the principals whom teachers described in our study varied their data-gathering *procedures*. In fact, the guidelines described by Acheson and Gall (1997) for use in a wide variety of settings are generally consistent with approaches identified in our data. They include, for example, the use of the following techniques:

- Selective verbatim (e.g., word-for-word transcriptions used for examining teacher questions, feedback, structuring statements, and classroom management)

- Observational records based on seating charts (e.g., for examining students' at-task behaviors, verbal flow, and movement patterns)
- Wide-lens techniques (e.g., use of anecdotal records, script taping, video and audio recordings, and journal writing)
- Checklists and timeline coding (e.g., pupil observation surveys, student questionnaires; checklists for question-and-answer teaching, lecture-explanation teaching; interaction analysis; timeline coding; observation systems; and teacher evaluation rating scales)

Acheson and Gall (1997) discuss other techniques similar to those used by the principals in our study for conducting feedback conferences (e.g., eliciting the teacher's opinions) and for using direct and indirect styles of supervision (e.g., listening more, talking less, ask clarifying questions, and providing verbal support).

In addition, our data indicate that principals who use effective approaches to instructional leadership frequently consider Hunter's (1980) conference types before proceeding with a conference:

Conference Type A: For first conference or with a fearful teacher; to bring *effective* behaviors to consciousness

Conference Type B: To generate a *variety* of teaching behaviors

Conference Type C: To find ways to *change* methods so as to improve on unsatisfactory parts of the lesson

Conference Type D: To *inform* a teacher of unfavorable teaching performance and to *suggest* alternative behaviors

Conference Type E_x: To stimulate continuing professional development of *excellent* teachers

Conference Type E: At the end of a series of instructional conferences (*evaluation*)

Research on Instructional Conferences

Although noteworthy knowledge and guidelines for principals' approaches to the conference exist, little systematic research on the instructional conference has been published. This fact and recent commentary in the professional literature (Holland, 1989) have generated renewed interest in studying *verbal interaction* in conferences. The resulting small body of research, produced primarily during the last two decades, indicates that instructional conferences are typically dominated by supervisors and encompass narrow concerns (Zimpher, deVoss, & Nott, 1980); provide short, prescriptive feedback to teachers (Blumberg & Cusick, 1970); threaten teacher self-esteem and self-determination (Roberts, 1992a); reveal gender differences regarding power, behavior, and control (Kraft, 1991); show unequal power relationships (Retallick, 1990; Roberts, 1992b); and lack teacher reflection and self-evaluation (Gitlin, Ogawa, & Rose, 1984; Zeichner & Liston, 1985). Several writers have argued that such power-related issues as well as other issues may best be approached through critical practices of instructional supervision (Bates, 1984; Foster, 1986; Smyth, 1985, 1988, 1990).

In a recent study, Blase and Blase (1996) explored the micropolitical (i.e., power) elements inherent in interactions between practicing supervisors and teachers in *successful* postobservation instructional conferences. An inductive analysis of data revealed four major micropolitical strategies used by conference participants: personal orientations (e.g., cognitive and affective frameworks of participants, interpersonal history, and individual agendas), conversational congruence (e.g., shared meanings, assumptions, credibility), formal authority, and situational variables (e.g., time, place, resources, and topic control). We concluded that attaining *deep reflection* and *free exchange* in conference situations—recognized goals of the instructional conference (Garman, 1990)—are, at best, difficult to achieve and are profoundly complicated by, for example, how participants use power to achieve their goals.

Indeed, research has confirmed that the instructional conference is frequently authoritarian and bureaucratic in nature, and this has been attributed, in part, to the hierarchical nature of authority associated with the position of the supervisor. Such a perspective assumes that the *supervisor's technical proficiency*—contrived, mechanical, and intentional use of techniques such as empathy, positive openings to verbal responses, conference analysis, and evaluation systems—rather than the teacher's *collaboration*—based on authentic interaction (an alternative to supervisor control)—leads to teacher growth and development (Holland, 1989).

Studies of Teacher Reflection

Contemporary studies of teacher reflection and engagement have also contributed to our understanding of the instructional conference. Retallick (1990), for example, analyzed conference discourse using a critical inquiry method, that is, "depth hermeneutics." He described supervisors' and teachers' talk during postobservation conferences focusing on interaction in earlier conferences. This talk constituted a useful form of "reflection on reflection," targeting participants' language and communication structures and, in turn, improving future conference interaction.

In related work, Zeichner and Liston (1985) expanded van Manen's (1977) and Schön's (1983) thinking about teacher reflection and Habermas's (1968/1978) idea about analytic, hermeneutic, and critical reasoning. Zeichner and Liston (1985) employed philosophical rather than theoretical methods to study practical reasoning during instructional conferences. Their work and empirical studies of conferences have revealed *dismally low levels* of reflection, reasoning, critical inquiry, and symmetrical communication in instructional conference interaction (Roberts, 1992b). (See Chapter 4 for more about reflection.)

In summary, research in this area has raised serious questions about the conference's contribution to collegiality and teacher growth (Roberts, 1994). These studies also explicate the importance of collaborative structures for teacher growth (Grimmett & Crehan, 1992) and suggest that social and political factors often dramatically undermine conference success (Hargreaves, 1990; St. Maurice, 1987).

The Need for Further Research

Anderson (1989) has suggested that the effects of instructional supervision on teacher classroom behavior require further study, and Waite (1995) has mentioned several foci for research (primarily sociocultural) in the area of supervisory interaction that have rich implications for practice. In fact, with respect to the supervisory conference, often the focal point of supervisor-teacher interaction regarding classroom instruction, recent research has described the logic and substance of supervisor-teacher discourse, difficulties that aspiring supervisors face when conducting instructional conferences, and the usefulness of conversation analysis and discourse analysis for exploring related problems. Such work has also addressed the developmental needs of supervisors, particularly those in training (Retallick, 1990; Roberts [now Blase], 1988, 1989a, 1989b, 1989c, 1991b, 1994; Waite, 1992; Zeichner & Liston, 1985).

Nevertheless, given the scarcity of studies exploring interpretation as an aspect of the conferences, and the relative imbalance of theory versus thorough systematic research on the supervisory conference, Holland (1989) has called for more and varied research, including the use of qualitative methods to explore the conferencing phenomenon. Furthermore, Pajak and Glickman (1989) have made similar recommendations based on Fishbein and Ajzen's (1975) paradigm of "who says what, how, to whom, with what effects?"

For example, more research is needed on the strategies, goals, purposes, and consequences of social and political interaction in the instructional conference and changes in conference interaction over time (i.e., in conferences held *after* the first instructional conference between a given supervisor and teacher). Research that compares and contrasts conferences with regard to participant experience, ethnicity, gender, class, and language is also needed. More broadly, studies focusing on instructional conferences in the context of the organizational, social, cultural, academic, and political milieu of the school would be valuable. In addition, investigations into elements of successful conferences (e.g., the supervisor's preparation and skills and, more important, the participants' interpretation of power/political strategies) should be initiated. Without question, the dearth of research in the areas noted above hinders us, in part, from becoming more effective as we work with teachers.

On a practical level, aspiring principals would benefit from university programs that provide at least fundamental academic preparation in micropolitical knowledge and skills. Such preparation could focus on building awareness in participants of the broad range of strategic interactions that occur in conferences and the consequences of these actions. For instance, prospective and practicing supervisors should become cognizant of their own everyday political orientations. An understanding of the importance of trust, respect, and support as well as the nature of professional collaboration and reflection would also be helpful in creating effective supervisory practice. More micropolitical knowledge could be acquired by observing conferences in an interactive mode and developing awareness of the interplay of strategies, purposes, and consequences.

Perhaps most important, instructional supervisors should be provided with opportunities to develop awareness of the differences between control-oriented strategies and empowerment strategies. Most supervisors are prepared to use only standard evaluation systems and mandated procedures that encourage them to assume a control orientation as opposed to a growth, collaborative, empowering orientation based on nonthreatening classroom observation and data gathering (Blase & Blase, 1996). For example, to reduce the negative effects of a control orientation, supervisors should learn to focus on the *effects* of supervisory behavior on *teacher performance and student achievement.* Because current school restructuring efforts emphasize collegiality and power sharing, knowledge of both control and empowerment will be especially crucial. Without such knowledge and relevant skill, supervisors may inadvertently undermine attempts to build new and dynamic forms of collegial, professional interaction in public schools; this is a problem merely compounded by such factors as poor preparation of teachers and principal overload, which forces leaders into a "survival mode."

The need for thoughtful conversation about teaching and learning implies that we address in our research and practice the prerequisites for autonomous behaviors of reflection on classroom behavior, application of understandings, and selection of teaching strategies to enhance student learning. Costa and Garmston (1994) include in these *states of mind* teachers' efficacy, flexibility, precision, consciousness, and interdependence. Unfortunately, empirical research in these areas is dismally sparse.

Zeroing In on Research About Principal-Teacher Discourse

Interestingly, conference interaction is being studied, in a limited way, through discourse analysis. The study of discourse (or talk and interaction) has historically taken place in anthropology, linguistics, semiotics, poetics, psychology, sociology, and communication research. In education, scholars have studied discourse from the perspectives of sociolinguistics, psycholinguistics, ethnomethodology, the sociology of language, educational psychology, the philosophy of language, computational linguistics, and narrative inquiry (Green & Wallat, 1981). Specifically, discourse analysis has been used as a heuristic to study the patterns and practical problems of communication in supervisory conferences based on classroom interaction. It has also been used to investigate other principal-teacher verbal interactions. Recent studies by Blase and Blase (1996), Roberts (1992a, 1992b), and Waite (1992) confirm the usefulness of discourse analysis and also suggest the intriguing possibility of linking social and linguistic dimensions of these types of interactions. Again, however, limited research exists in this area of inquiry.

Our Findings

Our data reveal that good principals used five primary conference strategies (also used in other instructional interactions), including (1) making suggestions, (2) giving feedback, (3) modeling, (4) using inquiry, and (5) soliciting advice and opinions.

Strategy 1: Food for Thought: Making Suggestions

We found that making suggestions—proactively giving advice for the improvement of instruction—was one central and powerful element of principals' verbal interaction with teachers. Principals made suggestions to teachers both during postobservation conferences *and* informally, in day-to-day interactions. In contrast to formal postobservation conference feedback, a reactive response to only what principals observed in the classroom, suggestions are often given proactively. They are designed to go beyond simple feedback to expand the teacher's instructional performance and students' learning.

In terms of discourse analysis, both suggestions and requests are considered "imperative" verbal forms used *to get someone to do something*. However, a supervisor making a suggestion assumes no special authority over the teacher, in contrast to the authority assumed by the giver of an order, demand, plea, or request. Even so, Roberts (1994) found (and we have confirmed in our present study) that

> the teacher's acceptance or rejection of a principal's "suggestion" is partially dependent on the teacher's view of the *fit* between the suggestion and the students' needs (which is related to the teacher's reflection on practice) as well as on the teacher's perception of his or her *ability to enact the suggestion*. Failing to address these concerns may preclude translation of the preferred suggestion (or discovered solution) into action. (p. 151, emphasis added)

Put another way, we found that teachers view a supervisor's suggestion as a valid request for action (i.e., not insulting, joking, or simply irrelevant) and respond to it positively when the following conditions are present:

- The suggested action is *purposeful* and appropriate to a perceived need.
- The teacher is *able* to perform (or has been taught how to perform) the action.
- The teacher is *not offended* by the suggestion. (For example, a teacher who already knows the solution to an instructional problem or knows how to improve his or her teaching but who is not given the opportunity to disclose it or arrive at it by reflection may be offended by a suggestion.)

Goals in Making Suggestions

In the following pages we examine our findings about principals' goals in giving suggestions to teachers, how suggestions are made effectively, and the effects of making suggestions for teachers.

Teachers in our study overwhelmingly reported that *good* principals' primary goal when making suggestions was

- *To improve teaching and learning*
  Her goal is to provide the very best learning environment for every child!

Other goals discussed were as follows:

- *To prevent teacher complacency and overreliance on traditional ("tried-and-true") instructional methods and to encourage creativity and innovation in instruction*
  The goal is to move faculty beyond their individual comfort zones or traditional methods.
  The goal is to encourage interactive learning instead of 100% lecture and passive student reception.
  The goal is to help us become more creative.
  The goal is to increase excitement and interest for the students . . . to make the instructional environment more inviting to students.

- *To create a supportive work environment and to avoid any form of criticism*

  I believe she wants the staff at my school to feel at home, like you feel with your family.

- *To help solve problems*

  In conferencing with my principal he offers suggestions to help "troubleshoot" problems relating to my classroom instruction.

How Do Good Principals Make Suggestions?

We discovered that good principals made purposeful, appropriate, nonthreatening suggestions characterized by the following elements:

1. Principals *listened* before making suggestions.

He listens to my ideas and provides input. He makes a point to pull the chair up to my desk and gives me his full attention.

She listens to me and treats me as a peer.

He listens to our concerns and tries to assist us in any way possible.

My principal is very appreciative of what we do. She is also very understanding and supportive and listens when we need to vent frustrations.

He would listen while I shared an upcoming unit, state that it was a great idea, and offer additional ideas to enhance my lessons.

2. Principals often made suggestions in such a way as to *extend*, broaden, or enrich teachers' thinking and strengths.

She commends me on a teaching strategy and then offers some other ideas in which to *extend* what I've done.

She always sees the positive aspect of the lesson. If there are areas for improvement, she would always *build* on your strengths.

He constantly offered *additional ideas* and was willing to provide any support needed to make the unit a success.

3. When making suggestions, principals shared, among other things, their own professional *experiences* to encourage teacher reflection.

> She listens to my problems and then responds in a way that makes me really think about things. She asks questions to get me to understand all aspects of a problem and then gives me *stories of her own experiences.*

> As a former math teacher, my principal *shares from his years of experience* what he considers to be different ways of teaching various topics. Because we share the same subject, it is easy to accept any suggestions he has for my classroom.

4. Principals indirectly made suggestions for the improvement of teaching through *examples and demonstrations.*

> My principal *showed me how* to ask "different" types of questions that got the students to respond more often. She also went over my quizzes and tests and showed me how to make sure my questions met the objectives by forming specific question items.

> She emphasizes learning styles a lot. She *gives examples* of ways that a particular concept or skill can be taught to children with different learning styles. She also realizes and addresses the fact that teachers have different teaching styles.

> My principal *shared an effective method* on how to improve student retention through review and participation.

> She *shows me* different things she did to motivate students.

5. Principals gave teachers *discretion,* or choice, to accept or reject their suggestions, and this was considered critical to the success of making suggestions.

> She gives me advice but *stands behind me* no matter what I choose to do. That's important!

6. At times, principals even supported instructional changes that *contradicted* current policy: In these cases, such changes resulted from both the principal's suggestion and the teacher's thinking.

My principal visited a class I was teaching [in which] I was using a sentence strategy program required by the department. The program stated I should question students rapid-fire, calling each by name and then asking the question. After the class, the principal said that it might be more effective if I asked the question and then waited a moment before calling on a student by name. He insisted that my questioning technique should change *despite the fact* that the old way was required by the department. I agreed that his method of questioning was a better one.

7. Principals bolstered their suggestions by encouraging teachers to *take risks* to improve instruction.

He encourages his teachers to try new things in the classroom. At faculty meetings he tells us to use a variety of teaching strategies. He stresses that *it's OK to try something* and learn it doesn't work for us as long as we TRY! He gave us "I tried" passes once to turn in to him when we tried something new. We indicated on them whether the thing we tried worked or bombed. After a whole year of working to integrate the computer lab into my classes, he gave me a certificate of appreciation for all my work even though some of my labs bombed!

8. Principals indirectly supplemented making suggestions by *distributing literature* on effective instruction (see Chapter 3 for more on the use of professional literature).

My principal uses notes as well as verbal reminders about things that create an effective classroom. When he wanted to encourage bell-to-bell teaching, he sent *articles* that described the types of improvements that come from this.

9. In most cases, principals' suggestions were given in face-to-face interactions. However, suggestions were also made in *writing* and typically accompanied by acknowledgment of a teacher's strengths and accomplishments.

She'll give *verbal and written praise* of certain aspects of lessons or the classroom environment . . . and also add suggestions to make them even better.

10. Principals worked to create a *culture* of instructional improvement throughout their schools by maintaining a focus on effective instructional methods and current educational research in both formal and informal interactions with teachers.

> There is a continuing *focus on improving instruction* through the principal's encouragement of use of a variety of methodologies and on incorporating the use of more technology. This is accomplished through formal faculty meetings and formal and informal conferences with both individuals and teams.

Finally, we found that in addition to the suggestions principals gave to teachers, the latter often *solicited* suggestions from principals in informal and formal situations:

> I feel free to discuss my teaching with my principal and informally *ask for advice.*

> She shares ideas about strategies when teachers *express a need* for help.

The Effects of Making Suggestions

You will see below that principals' suggestions strongly enhance teacher reflection and reflectively informed instructional behavior. Our data indicate that teachers implemented new ideas, used greater variety in teaching, responded to student diversity, prepared and planned more carefully, took more risks, achieved better focus, and used professional discretion to make changes. Teachers also reported positive effects on motivation, satisfaction, self-esteem, confidence, sense of security, and feelings of being supported:

> In teaching measurement to first graders, I needed to think about "real-life" situations in order to bring my students' learning to a level of synthesis. My principal gave me some ideas on how to do this, which I will consider next year. She helps me *look at my teaching through the eyes of another.*

> His reminders have *made me realize* that when I don't teach bell-to-bell, I am losing valuable time. I changed my behavior and try to make better use of time.

She gave me actual examples of good teaching lessons, of teaching strategies, and how one can be creative in the classroom and teach at the same time. I am always *looking for new ideas* to use and pass on to others. I don't like to be repetitive with stale ideas that tend to lose their impact.

It is great to consider what other teachers in our school are doing, both successfully and unsuccessfully. I can be *more creative*. I may decide something won't work for me, but I respect her [the principal] enough to consider something could work for me.

I have become so much *more aware* of the modes that children learn best in. I now understand the reasoning behind this and have firsthand observations that teaching to learning styles works. I always try to include in my lesson plans visual, auditory, and tactile ideas on everything I teach.

I can use my classroom in an *experimental* way. I can try new ideas and not worry about constant evaluation. She wants me to feel free and open in the classroom.

I feel like this is a good strategy because it makes me *want to do more* for student learning. It [suggesting things] is done in a nonthreatening manner.

I felt *inspired*, I felt *supported*, I felt *safe*.

She makes me feel *confident* and *professional*. She treats me as an equal.

I feel *supported, respected, energized*, and *uplifted*. It makes me feel like we're on the same side. I feel intellectually *stimulated* and expanded. He gets super results.

I feel that she has a true concern about all the children and how best to teach them, and it *motivates* me to have that same concern and to implement good strategies that work.

It is very effective. Personally, I am more *motivated* by suggestions than confrontation.

A Caveat

Some teachers we studied strongly approved of their principal's use of suggestion but with certain qualifications. A few reported that a particular form of suggestion (such as a direct challenge) "worked" for them, but they suspected it might "intimidate" other teachers ("He challenges us to really think about the reasons for curriculum decisions; this is a good strategy, but some might think it's a personal affront"). Others lamented that their principals relied too heavily on suggestion alone and failed to acknowledge the importance of other leadership strategies ("She needs to be in the classroom more, too").

Strategy 2: Holding Up the Mirror: Giving Feedback

By visiting classrooms and subsequently giving feedback to teachers, good principals hope to "hold up a mirror," to be simply "another set of eyes," or to be a "critical friend" who engages in thoughtful discourse with the teacher about what was observed.

The Principals' Goals in Giving Feedback

Teachers reported that principals' goals in providing them with postobservation feedback included enhancing their motivation and morale ("He is trying to promote good morale") as well as improving school climate ("He wants to create an open and comfortable climate for the teacher and the students"). Such goals notwithstanding, the bulk of our data point out that good principals emphasized the goal of *instructional* improvement:

Feedback allows you to *think* and reevaluate your strategies.

He wants to make us aware of the *importance* of our actions by letting us know of our influence on these kids.

My administrator's motto is "student success." He likes children to feel *successful.*

He wants us to be flexible and gear activities to the instructional and social needs of our population.

He's trying to keep the goal of educational *success* fresh in our minds.

To encourage *critical thinking* in the building.

The principal plans to keep teachers *on task* and make certain that we teach the students.

Providing the *best possible instruction* in a safe, healthy environment and attempting to "save" all of the children is the number one priority of my principal.

She wanted me to begin to *look at my classroom* situation differently.

His interest is in *school improvement.* He has faith that I will implement the new program if I think it will be effective.

When principals provided teachers with direct feedback regarding classroom observations, they were being *reactive*, responding descriptively and interpretively to only what they observed. We found that *effective feedback* had several elements:

1. Whether *written* (on formal observation or evaluation forms) or oral, feedback during conferences frequently included explanatory comments and tended to focus specifically on behavior observed in the classroom. For example, one teacher reported,

> When conferencing with me after observing in my class, he always *reads his notes* to me about what I was doing during the observation. He interjects comments like "good" and other positive remarks about the specific teaching incidents he observed. He makes no negative remarks at all concerning my teaching.

2. Good principals attempted to be as nonevaluative and *nonjudgmental* as possible in giving postobservation feedback in conferences. This, along with the expression of sincere caring, interest, and support, further ameliorated the possible negative effects of formal evaluation for teachers:

> She is a *very positive* administrator and readily *encourages* her teachers. After completing the state observation, she confers with us on an individual basis to explain her evaluation comments. She is *approachable* with an open-door policy.

3. Principals' substantive feedback was "detailed" and "descriptive," and addressed the positive aspects of what they observed. *Constructive criticism* was given in an open and diplomatic manner; nevertheless, it was given infrequently:

Mr. Smith makes no *negative* comments at all.

[My principal] usually chooses a very public place (nonthreatening) to give advice or an evaluation. He tempers any *constructive criticism* with a great deal of praise—a definite plus. Our first conferences focused on improving my processes: grading consistency, week-by-week formats, etc. Hence, he didn't make me feel as though I lacked the necessary intelligence to do the job, only the experience.

4. Principals *praised* teachers throughout postobservation conferences whether they gave positive descriptive feedback or constructive criticism (see Chapter 6 for more about praise):

He always *ends with praise.*

During my evaluation she was extremely positive in her feedback. She gave me a lot of *praise,* which I needed to hear, being a first-year teacher.

The principal wrote a note at the bottom of the evaluation form that said, "You are a *credit* to the teaching profession." In our conference he asked if he could send other teachers to observe my classroom.

She *praised* my attempts to try new ideas in the classroom. When they were not effective, she didn't make me feel like I had failed.

5. In addition, principals' approach to postobservation conferences tended to be *collaborative.* That is, in giving feedback, principals attempted to establish collegial relationships with teachers based on trust, respect, two-way interaction, and a problem-solving orientation:

He's *open* to ideas . . . wants to hear what I think.

When we have postobservation conferences, he describes what he has seen. Interestingly enough, he tends to select the things that I too think are important. I think I have influenced him in listening for types of questions, follow-up questions, and so on. I've worked for him a long time and *we've spent hours discussing good teaching.* He's very open to ideas. After he has given his positive comments, he usually tries to make a suggestion for something to try such as attention to wait time.

My principal is *collaborative* in her conferencing. Rather than telling me where I could use improvement, she *asks me* what I feel went well or not so well with my lesson. I find that I dominate most of the conversations. She is able to generate with me methods for improvement . . . I look forward to her visits as a chance to grow.

6. Good principals made themselves *available* to discuss feedback with teachers subsequent to the conference:

He has an open-door policy. I can always go to him after a conference and bounce ideas off of him once I initiate the conversation.

7. Although principal feedback usually emphasized teacher performance, principals also responded to *students'* academic and social *behavior*:

My principal is quite specific about the *effects* my actions have on students. During our conferences he will tell me that my discussion with a child had positively impacted him/her.

My principal at one time came into my classroom and observed my class during center work. She found that many traffic problems as well as behavior problems were occurring because the closet of art supplies and my art center were on opposite sides of the room. *Fixing this* helped me significantly.

In evaluating my discipline plans for an ADD student, we [my principal and I] discussed *possibilities* to motivate the student to want to complete his work.

8. Principals also provided feedback on the *teacher-student relationship* itself:

She *compliments* me on the rapport I have with the children.

Impact on Teachers

Although postobservation feedback produced many effects on teachers, the more prominent ones were on reflection and reflectively informed teacher behavior. *Reflectively informed behaviors* refer to implementing new ideas, using greater variety in instruction, responding to student diversity, planning more carefully, and achieving better focus. In addition, teachers reported that postobservation feedback had positive effects on motivation, self-esteem, confidence, and sense of security:

> I was able to change the instructional delivery method I used in a social studies lesson. This strategy [postconference feedback] offered *more hands-on* activities, and I was also able to *incorporate other* suggested real-life strategies into the lesson.

> This type of strategy builds my *confidence*. My supervisor reinforces the fact that I am, in fact, a teacher. As I collaborate with her, I learn more about my teaching. I look forward to her next visit as a chance to grow. The *confidence* I have described shows in my teaching. As I gain positive feedback, I *continue* using what works in the classroom. And because I do not fear negative evaluation, I am willing to take *risks*.

> I am more *willing to try* various activities that might be considered a little extreme because I know I will be supported and I know I can make it work for the kids. He wants us to be the best possible teachers we can. I like taking chances and being bold, not like the other teachers in my field. With his support I feel very comfortable doing just that.

> I feel more *confident* in what I teach and how I teach it. I am more *relaxed*; therefore, I am able to put a lesson together quicker and more precisely. People tend to work harder when they receive positive feedback.

> He made me *feel good about myself* and my teaching and inspired me to look for ways to stay on top of current topics and to think about what I did well and figure out what can be done better. I was more confident when I went into the classroom. I was *committed* to displaying these good techniques daily.

I like getting a pat on the back. It's genuine. It *encourages me to continue* to do a good job. I feel my principal is very aware of what is happening in my room. It's supportive.

I plan to use this strategy myself when I become a supervisor. It has so many *positive* outcomes that stem from it.

She is a motivating *role model* and a *mentor* in my endeavors to become an administrator.

It should be noted that a few teachers felt slightly manipulated. These teachers viewed their principals' use of postobservation feedback as positive, but they questioned the authenticity of this feedback: "This strategy is good, but sometimes I feel manipulated. I just feel that he tries to say something positive because he thinks he should. It's hard to know how he really feels."

Strategy 3: Principal Modeling

Several teachers reported that their principals, on occasion, actually taught during classroom visits in order to model good instruction. Such modeling was not considered intrusive because the principals had cultivated respectful and trusting relationships with teachers. Modeling (like making suggestions and giving feedback) was in fact viewed as an impressive example of instructional leadership, one that yielded very positive effects on teacher reflection and reflectively informed behavior:

The principal *models* positive interactions with students and by his responses and questions of them continuously reminds me of the need to provide many different approaches to instruction/learning and to keep my mind open to children's individual lives and needs.

My principal utilizes a great deal of informal *"coaching" and mentoring.* He is in and out of the entire faculty's classes. I value his insights because he was an excellent teacher. His love of children and young people was so obvious that we trusted him somehow . . . . Often he asks if he could teach a class. Watching him is a joy. I honestly believe I did some of my best reflecting after talking with or watching this man teach.

Sometimes principal modeling occurred during interactions with teachers *outside of the classroom*:

My principal showed me *how to ask* "different" types of questions that got the students to respond more often. It helped me to be more student-focused. She also went over my quizzes and tests and showed me how to make sure my questions met the objectives by forming specific question items.

Strategy 4: Using Inquiry

We also found that good principals usually took an inquiry approach to talk with teachers: This approach included "behavior whose purpose is to learn what others think, know, want, or feel" (Bolman & Deal, 1991, p. 138):

He asks many *questions* regarding my methods. The formal evaluation was used and our postconference session was very informal. He directly used an inquiry method.

In each postconference to an observation my instructional supervisor will close with the *question*, "What do you think you could have done better?"

The principal, in observing what is taking place in my room, will *ask me questions* about why I am doing what I am doing, or what my intended outcomes are. This encourages me to be reflective about what I do. She rarely has a suggestion, but her questions cause me to evaluate what I do.

(See Chapter 4 for a discussion of how inquiry spurs *reflection*.)

Strategy 5: Soliciting Advice and Opinions

Our study demonstrates that good principals solicited teachers' *advice and opinions* about classroom instruction, and such advice and opinions enhanced their instructional leadership role in the school:

> She often *asks my advice* on a particular problem. Later she tells me she is going to *suggest my solution to others.*

Principals also solicited advice from the teachers they attempted to influence and gave them *discretion* in responding to their advice.

> She presented me with information on a gifted program that she wanted me to consider and asked my advice. She told how money would be available to complete the course work necessary. She *left it up to me* to decide whether I could make use of the program in my teaching.

We found that soliciting advice primarily affected teacher motivation and self-esteem and, to a lesser degree, teachers' reflection and reflectively informed behavior:

> Seeking my advice caused me to feel *valued* as an instructor. This increased my *confidence* in my teaching ability. I am *motivated* to do more.

> He asks for my advice in designing new programs of instructional strategies. As I study the new strategies/programs, I become *motivated* to try these new theories of learning. I become more *enthusiastic.* My enthusiasm causes me to spend more time developing lessons and strategies. My enthusiasm influences the student.

> Our principal frequently seeks my opinion in planning. It makes me feel that *ideas I have are valid.* Her excitement about my ideas is catching. By asking me for my input or ideas, I feel *valued.*

> I am appreciative that my principal seeks my opinion on opportunities for growth in teaching. This has made me more attentive to possible needs. The openness of my principal allows me to feel comfortable in discussing needs in the classroom and has helped to *eliminate any stress* I might feel concerning my evaluation as a teacher. This process gave me a part in decision making. . . . I could claim ownership in that it was something I wanted to

do. This strategy gives me a *feeling of worth* and I think that's important.

Asking for my advice makes me *feel important* as a teacher and as a person. It makes me feel even more important when the principal follows my advice. It's very motivating.

The Bad News

Earlier we indicated that our study also investigated characteristics (e.g., strategies, behaviors, attitudes, goals) of principals whom teachers viewed as *ineffective* instructional leaders and the adverse effects they had on classroom instruction. Among other things, teachers criticized such principals for their failings with regard to formal observations and evaluation. First, teachers reported that some principals had *no formal observation or evaluation process in place*:

My principal *does not use* a systematic, formal evaluation procedure for the teachers in our building and also gives very little informal feedback or support for individual teacher professional growth.

In addition, in schools with such processes, ineffective instructional leaders were blamed for *not conducting* postobservation conferences:

At the end of the year the principal dropped a memo in my mailbox that said: *"No conference required."* I was to come by the office to sign my annual evaluation from.

Other ineffective principals, according to our data, *failed to complete* postobservation forms:

She has no idea what goes on. She observed me four weeks ago and *still has not filled out the form* or given me feedback. I asked for it two weeks ago and got nothing. Yesterday she asked me to *fill it out myself.*

Moreover, teachers explained that ineffective principals who did conduct postobservation conferences frequently *failed to provide* any growth-promoting constructive feedback about their observations in classrooms:

> My instructional supervisor came into my room once this year to assess me, gave me a good rating, told me there was *nothing* she saw that I needed to work on, and *left*.

> Evaluation conferences are not too effective. The principal hates to critique people negatively. Oddly enough, you get a negative disposition because you *haven't been challenged to improve*.

> I really wish my principal and I could get specific feedback about my teaching; it makes it harder to improve if you *don't know where to go*.

As a result of this practice, teachers described postobservation conferences as a "sham," and they viewed their principals as "insincere."

> He observes my class for my evaluation, then leaves a form in my box for me to sign. He has *never discussed* my teaching with me. Even though my evaluations have all been excellent, evaluations like that are very negative. They seem *insincere*. Evaluation days are also the only times he sees my classroom.

> Even though the formal, written evaluation is positive and complimentary, his flat affect, lack of enthusiasm, and lack of interaction with me lend an air of *hypocrisy* to his written comments.

A few teachers noted that their ineffective principals gave *all* teachers positive feedback despite glaring differences in performance:

> Our principal is *positive with all of us*. I see teachers doing what I know are not sound teaching practices, but I know they have positive observations too. Therefore, what is written on my evaluation form influences me very little. *I'm not certain if it is real*!

Some teachers complained that ineffective principals conducted postobservation conferences too *infrequently* ("once every three years is hardly adequate to have evaluation conferences"), and several teachers reported that postobservation conferences were entirely *punitive*:

> The principal *threatens* and tells *half truths*. He *bullies* and often *lies*. When conferencing with him, he is *not at all open*.

Like doing nothing (e.g., not making any informal class visits as mentioned earlier and as described more fully in Chapter 5), not holding *postobservation* conferences (certainly not an influence strategy) reflects a principal's unwillingness to engage in instructional leadership.

Principals' Goals

Most of the teachers who discussed poor postobservation conferences and evaluation could identify "no goals" with their ineffective principal's behavior: However, some believed that this problem resulted from "time constraints" or a principal's lack of interest. Several teachers reported that their principal only did the minimum required by formal evaluation systems to, as one teacher stated, "meet state and district requirements, nothing more."

The Effects of Poor Conferences

Ineffective postobservation conferences had powerful, negative effects on teachers. In addition to losing respect for and trust in their principals, teachers reported adverse effects on their motivation and self-esteem as well as substantial increases in anger and a sense of futility:

> Evaluations are insignificant and not a true reflection of my teaching. I *don't give much credit* to such overly positive evaluations, as they feel somewhat *insincere* to me.

> I want a supervisor to help me grow, *not* tell me that I cannot get any better. I don't think she has a clue to what I do in my classroom. I became *resentful*. I avoid her because I think *she is incompetent* in supervision.

The evaluation is a formality. Everyone (unless the administration is out to get them) gets pretty much the same evaluation. It's *meaningless*. It's a *waste of time*.

Class visits have become a *"show and tell"* experience. The evaluation process does not provide any feedback to change instructional methods. It makes some teachers *lazy* by making them feel there is no need for improvement, which is not true.

I feel I *lack support and guidance* from my principal in becoming a better teacher. I also *lack respect* for his leadership. I try to seek colleagues instead of my principal to share new ideas and thoughts and to have professional dialogues. Our principal lacks teacher respect for his leadership because he does not promote professional growth among staff members.

I figured, "Boy, she must be so busy that she *doesn't care* enough to talk to me." It made me shift to *neutral* in my teaching for awhile. I figured I'd just coast. This strategy promotes *low morale*.

I'm probably *not* really being treated as a *valued professional*. It makes me more "relaxed" (not always a good thing) in my teaching habits and style. It makes it harder to improve if you don't know where to go. I feel *frustrated* and in some ways angry. I want to improve. I feel like I'm *not worth her time*.

Another evaluation . . . all "satisfactory," *ho-hum*. It negates my motivation to grow.

I *wonder* if he really thinks I do a good job. I am hesitant to discuss pedagogical matters with him. It pisses me off that my students don't receive his recognition either.

(For more on the effects of wasting teachers' time and "abandoning" them, see Chapter 5.)

Summary

As a critical component of instructional leadership, the instructional conference should be positive, reflective, and motivating to a teacher. Our findings persuade us that solid efforts by principals along these lines can produce significant results for teachers' classroom performance. Conversely (as you have seen here and will see in later chapters), abandonment of teachers or an attitude of condescension on a principal's part can cause significant damage to teachers and, ultimately, the students with whom they work.

Staff Development: Promoting Professional Growth

The field of staff development is evolving gradually from a patchwork of courses and workshops into a system ensuring that education professionals regularly enhance their academic knowledge, professional performance, and image as professionals. . . . The study of academic substance, teaching, and school improvement should be an inescapable part of the job and . . . the organization should arrange and pay for the system.

Joyce & Showers, 1995, pp. 8-9

[Teachers need new work habits] that are collegial and public . . . not solo and private . . . a new way of learning about learning.

Meier, 1995, p. 140

Schools [must] structure themselves to support deeper forms of student and teacher learning.

Darling-Hammond, 1996, p. 5

[Information-literate citizens] are equipped to be lifelong learners because they know how to learn.

Hancock, 1993, p. 3

In this chapter we discuss another key aspect of good instructional leadership—staff development—and present specific findings from our study about what effective principals do to enhance staff development in their schools. We discuss the importance of the following:

- Emphasizing the *study of teaching and learning*
- Supporting *collaboration* among educators
- Developing *coaching* relationships among educators
- Using *action research* to inform instructional decision making
- Providing *resources* for redesign of programs
- Applying the *principles* of adult growth, learning, and development to all phases of the staff development program

In addition, we show that good staff development generally motivates teachers and enhances their self-esteem. Staff development also increases teacher reflection and reflectively informed behavior, including preparation and planning, risk taking, diversity in the classroom, and collaboration between and among teachers.

Research on Teaching and Learning

Effective Staff Development: What We Know

For more than a quarter of a century, Bruce Joyce, director of Booksend Laboratories in Pauma Valley, California, has been studying teachers' repertoires and synthesizing research on teaching models. He and his colleagues have produced valuable resources to help educators enhance their skills and to use varied, research-based strategies to help students learn. They have also reviewed the literature in the areas of curricula, teaching, learning, training, and staff development; they have conducted large-scale initiatives for school renewal; and they have completed research involving thousands of teachers, administrators, agencies, districts, states, organizations, and foreign countries.

From these sources, Joyce and his colleagues have produced solid evidence of the potential *effects of instructional innovations* such as teaching skills and technologies, and they have demonstrated these effects by using the most rigorous scientific methods, in the form of effect sizes (the difference between an experimental and a control group, computed in terms of standard deviations; see Glass, 1982, and Joyce & Calhoun, 1996, for more details).

Indeed, from volumes of data, extensive research, and many years of practice, Joyce and his colleagues produced a vision of an effective staff development system. His recent book with Beverly Showers, *Student Achievement Through Staff Development* (Joyce & Showers, 1995), deals with planning a comprehensive staff development system to support teaching and learning. The book also discusses the governance, design, and implementation of a system's elements and programs.

Generally speaking, we found that good principals frequently provided formal staff development *opportunities* to address emergent instructional *needs*, and doing so had a powerful effect on the teacher. Addressing teachers' needs made staff development *meaningful*. Several teachers explained,

> She sensed the uncertainty and tension among the primary-level faculty members and used staff development programs to *help us be more effective and confident* in our teaching.

> They [inservices] helped me to understand new concepts and implement them in the classroom. He tries hard to provide us with current *information based on our needs.* I already have a strong program and add the best parts of a new concept to my existing program.

> Staff development activities make me think he understands that we all need a jump start from time to time and are *anxious to learn.* He trusts my ability to learn new things and make the most of it. I share what I learn with my peers.

In addition, good principals used staff development programs to encourage instructional *innovation*:

> Her goals are to get more people to use *innovative methods* of instruction.

> Our principal provides a lot of appropriate staff development opportunities for all grade levels. I am the instructional lead teacher at our elementary school, and now have learned the

curriculum needs of teachers. I did not know that some teachers are terrified *to take risks* with different teaching strategies. Our principal has encouraged all of us to think about what we're doing, to take risks, to brainstorm, and use our planning time more effectively.

As a faculty, we had real concerns regarding reading instruction. I was uncomfortable with what was expected of me. We had changed the language arts series and were not given directions on implementation. Our principal *sensed our uncertainty*. After some inservice on reading instruction techniques, I felt more secure, and I could see an improvement with my students. I did alter my methods after the workshops.

According to our data, teacher *input* into the design and content of staff development, as well as *optional* attendance policies, increased its value:

My principal provides a lot of appropriate staff development opportunities for all grade levels and for all teachers. After one staff development session the presenter came back and *worked directly with teachers* over several months. This has been a wonderful help.

We are given a lot of opportunities to learn new strategies and new learning techniques at staff development meetings, many of which are optional. Our staff development always supports our major instructional goal, which we *all have input on*. We have a lot to say in what and how we want to do things.

Most of our staff development is optional. By giving us *voice and choice*, we are more motivated to go to inservices and learn new things that we can try out and actually use, instead of going to tons of meetings and never really having the time to try out new strategies.

Finally, the value of staff development sessions was often enhanced for teachers when principals themselves *participated*:

One of the most dynamic, full-of-impact strategies that my principal uses is to attend inservices and conferences *with us*! Whenever and whatever! We know she knows exactly how technology should be used in the classroom. I'm so impressed that she values this shared learning so much!

She attends inservices with us. This *partnership in training* has had a powerful impact on my personality. To truly see the investment she has made in us is extremely powerful and extremely motivating. I'm much more energized to try new things in my classroom. She believes in people and models this belief.

Teaching Models

Sound education requires a combination of personal, social, and academic learning by students. We believe that teachers should help students achieve such requisite knowledge and skill *through the use of combined teaching methods based on different teaching repertoires*. To illustrate, a teacher may use several repertoires: one instructional method for vocabulary learning and another for generating classroom practice in higher levels of thinking such as synthesis. The development of those repertoires forms the basis of effective staff development. In addition, we advocate that teachers gather data over time about students' cognitive development, social history, personality, and learning orientations. Then, *drawing on their repertoire of teaching models*, teachers can help students increase their learning aptitude.

Drawing on decades of research in the areas of curriculum, effective schools, teaching methods, effective teacher training, knowledge construction, and metacognition, researchers have recently attempted to bring order to education's "storehouse" of models of teaching (or, as some say, models for learning). In their book *Creating Learning Experiences: The Role of Instructional Theory and Research* (1996), Joyce and Calhoun identify four "families of models," each of which demonstrates effect sizes (e.g., the impacts of the models on student learning; see Figure 3.1). They discuss each family in terms of the types of student learning it promotes, as well as its orientation toward people and how they learn. Most important, the models they describe meet these criteria:

- *Practicability*, as refined by experience

Information-Processing Models
  Inductive thinking
  Concept attainment
  Scientific inquiry
  Inquiry training
  Cognitive growth
  Advance organizer
  Mnemonics
  Synectics

Social Models
  Group investigation
  Social inquiry
  Jurisprudential inquiry
  Laboratory method
  Role-playing
  Positive interdependence
  Structured social inquiry

Personal Models
  Nondirective teaching
  Awareness training
  Classroom meeting
  Self-actualization
  Conceptual systems

Behavioral Systems Models
  Social learning
  Mastery learning
  Programmed learning
  Simulation
  Direct teaching
  Anxiety reduction

Figure 3.1. Families of Teaching Models (See Joyce & Calhoun, 1996)

- *Adaptability* for various learning styles and subject matter
- Lifetime *utility,* or learning tools for life
- *Flexibility* across grade levels

The study of teaching and learning (i.e., concepts, models, and research findings) and the expansion of repertoires are primary and ongoing tasks of teachers. This means that the school is a learning environment for teachers as well as students, an environment that emphasizes lifelong learning and experimentation. Therefore, we recommend that school leaders use staff development to provide the following conditions for teachers to learn about, synthesize, and enact various teaching strategies via

- Opportunities to study the *literature* and *proven programs*
- *Demonstrations* of new skills
- *Practice* of new skills
- Support from *peer coaches*
- Assistance in studying student learning through *action research* (i.e., gathering data about student achievement)
- Assistance in studying how new strategies are *implemented* and how they *affect students*

An extensive discussion of teaching-learning models can be found in Joyce and Weil's *Models of Teaching* (1996). For highlights of current research on effective teaching and its relationship to the improvement of learning, see Waxman and Walberg (1991).

How Do Teachers Learn?
Principles That Shape Staff Development

Part and parcel of the design and implementation of staff development programs is an understanding of *principles of adult development* (e.g., relevance, autonomy, applicability) and the conditions that enhance adult learning. Phillips and Glickman (1991) have found, for example, that teachers who work in a stimulating and supportive environment can reach higher stages of development. Joyce and Showers (1995) have demonstrated that "virtually all teachers can learn the most powerful and complex teaching strategies, provided that staff development is designed properly" (p. 10). In contrast, the work of Glickman et al. (1995), which compares actual and optimal teacher development, shows that an oppressive school environment and traditional (e.g., bureaucratic, evaluation-oriented) approaches to supervision often hinder teacher development. To increase teacher

1. **Stages** (for teachers, see Oja & Pine)
   Cognitive (Piaget)
   Moral (Kohlberg)
   Conceptual (Hunt)
   Ego (Loevinger)
   Concern (Fuller)

2. **Life Cycle**
   Goals (Buhler)
   Critical issues (Erikson)
   Stability vs. transition (Levinson)

3. **Transitions** (for teachers, see Krupp)
   Critical events (Brim & Ryff)
   Stressful events (Fiske et al.)
   On time/off time (Neugarten)

4. **Role**
   Developmental tasks (Havighurst)
   Family, work, and self (Juhasz)
   Love, work, and learning (Merriam & Clark)

5. **Motivation** (Maslow, Herzberg)

Figure 3.2. Overview of Adult/Teacher Development Research/Theories Presented in *Supervision of Instruction* (Glickman, Gordon, & Ross-Gordon, 1995)

effectiveness, they propose that supervisors [principals] do the following:

- Adhere to the principles of *adult learning*
- Respond to and foster teachers' professional *stage* development
- Recognize and support different phases within teachers' *life cycles*
- Help teachers to understand, navigate, and learn from *life transition events*
- Recognize and accommodate teachers' various *roles,* and
- Enhance teacher *motivation*

(For an overview of related research summarized in Glickman et al., 1995, see Figure 3.2.)

Our Findings: The Lifelong
Study of Teaching and Learning

The hallmark of effective staff development is a philosophy of and support for *lifelong learning* about teaching and learning (Joyce & Showers, 1995). Below, we discuss how the principals described in our study *consistently* supported the study of teaching and learning throughout teachers' careers in several powerful ways. These included informing teachers of current trends and issues; encouraging attendance at workshops, seminars, and conferences; building a culture of collaboration and learning; promoting coaching; using inquiry to drive staff development; and providing resources to promote growth and redesign.

Following Current Trends and Issues

Good principals informed faculty members of *current trends* and *issues* to (1) foster innovation in teaching (methods, materials, technology) and (2) increase student learning. For example, one teacher reported:

> My principal wants to *stretch our thinking* so that new methods are tried. He wants you to be the best that you can be and he wants the kids to learn as much as they can.

Often, principals distributed educational journal *articles* containing information relevant to classroom teaching and the specific *needs and interests* of teachers:

> She will say, "I know you're really interested in new techniques and innovations in language arts. I saw these *articles* and thought you might be interested. If you decide any of these would be good to use in your classroom, let me know. I'd like to discuss your trials and see what you think."

> He knew that I was interested in proactive discipline plans. So, as he read professional literature, he would copy *articles* he thought I would be interested in reading. I would skim the article. If something caught my attention, I would use the concepts or ideas

in my classroom. I would sometimes share the concepts with regular education teachers to support instruction and discipline throughout the school. Sometimes articles provided support to implement new programs.

Less frequently, a principal would distribute articles to a whole faculty with an *invitation to discuss* them with the principal or with other teachers:

My principal sends out a weekly staff bulletin. Attached to each bulletin is an educational article from a journal pertaining to specific teaching strategies. We as teachers are encouraged to read these and *discuss* them with the principal if fitting. It's nice to read these because they introduce me to new ideas, and this helps me reflect on my own teaching. My principal is helping me grow using a very nonthreatening technique.

Throughout the year my principal places in our mailboxes copies of *articles* relating to instructional effectiveness. She will occasionally address specific issues in faculty meetings or in individual conferences. What makes her method effective with me is the respect she shows by assuming we can read and can take what applies to our class. She is very knowledgeable regarding the effectiveness of a variety of instructional strategies so I realize what she places in our mailboxes has value.

The *effects* of sharing professional and research literature with teachers were usually very positive and included increases in teacher motivation, reflection on teaching and learning, and reflectively informed instructional behavior. For example, in terms of the latter, examination of the current literature helped teachers bring more instructional variety ("to get out of the rut") and innovation to the classroom:

My principal takes time to do research for us. When she hands me an article, it makes me stop and *rethink* what I'm currently doing in my classroom. It reminds me that it's good to make changes every so often. This year, one of the articles was about keeping portfolios for math students. I had been feeling frustrated about the fact that so many students lack basic skills. So, I'm keeping portfolios for every student and charting their progress as we go. This has given students something tangible to prove that they have been successful at something. Teachers are so busy doing what has to be done that we tend to let ourselves get "stale" as teachers.

Articles have led to a consideration of a *variety* of teaching methods and the research that supports each one. It has led to conversations with other teachers regarding classroom application. It has led to others adopting cooperative learning strategies I use. Her competence as a leader adds value to the information she gives us to consider. Teachers are expected to do all they can to facilitate student achievement, but are not expected to lower standards or give grades.

The exposure to new ideas is refreshing. It *motivates* me to put in a bit more effort. I am willing to introduce new strategies . . . and varied methods. It helps prevent getting "stuck in a rut."

This literature *motivates* me to learn more. . . . It develops more awareness of different approaches to use. I have switched from basal readers to all trade books. I now place more of an emphasis on vocabulary, reading, comprehension, and other skills.

These articles make me *aware* of what I'm doing for kids. I think, Will these ideas be beneficial in the classroom? These articles are really helpful because I want to do what's best for kids, and I like new ideas.

Articles she distributes *encourage* me to stay current and try new things and to use a variety of techniques in my classroom. I know my principal is really interested in what worked best with my kids. I frequently try new strategies or work to improve an old one. I can do different things and be OK with that. This strategy is effective because it is nonthreatening—I have a choice about what I use from the articles, if anything.

This strategy [of providing articles] gets me *searching* new and innovative things on my own. I am constantly thinking about innovative and creative things I can try with my classes and the rest of the staff regarding technology; they are often outcome-based things that please my principal.

Our principal often shared articles he thought might be useful. For example, an article on discipline caused me to *reflect* on my teaching behavior and schoolwide discipline methods. Teachers formed a schoolwide discipline committee that was described in a particular article, and discipline was improved. We did not feel that we had to use the information he gave us; we just selected what we needed.

At times, principals distributed educational literature to teachers to further their own instructional agendas—"to get across ideas he wanted to get across"—with positive results:

She provides research articles to read in order for me to *"buy into"* a concept. She also lets me lead the concept into schoolwide action. She knows I am an innovative teacher and taps into that knowledge to introduce new concepts into the school environment. This motivates me and other teachers to learn new things.

Encouraging Attendance at Workshops, Seminars, and Conferences

Good principals provided teachers with information about and encouraged them to attend workshops, seminars, and conferences related to instruction. Occasionally they were able to fund attendance. Principals did not pressure, but encouraged, teachers to attend; they permitted teachers to "choose" whether or not to attend. In general, principals stressed the goal of instructional innovation:

She *informs* me of innovative seminars and workshops and offers to send me if I choose.

Dr. B often *suggests or informs* me of various conferences, visitations, observations, and professional meetings that I might be interested in, and then helps to make arrangements for me to attend in the way of stipends, fees, or substitute coverage.

She provides school *funds* to help us attend workshops we are interested in attending.

He offers college *credit* for classes that better your skills. These skills may not be directly related to what you teach but are skills that can make your classroom management a lot better or easier.

Although teachers reported that their participation in workshops, seminars, and conferences positively affected their self-esteem and sense of being supported, their motivation, classroom reflection, and reflectively informed behavior were affected most dramatically. Increases in innovation and variety of teaching methods in classrooms, for example, were discussed:

I *want to learn* new and more effective ways to engage students and increase learning by attending workshops. My principal is supportive of my natural need to learn new things. She cares enough about me to recognize my positive qualities and support me in fulfilling my need for growth.

I think that it is very important to keep abreast of trends and issues in my field. Workshops do that for me. I have tried several of the teaching strategies I have learned. Some work for me and some don't enhance my teaching. I am very *aware of all the resources* teachers have. My principal recognizes that I do not want to be just an ordinary teacher. I feel *proud and excited.*

I have learned a lot from extra training and workshops. I am *willing to implement* new material and techniques *and study* to stay abreast of recent developments.

By providing school funds to attend workshops, she makes me feel that she wants me to improve by trying new ideas. This makes me *try harder* to be the best teacher I can be. Her support sets high expectations and is very motivational for me.

My principal's encouragement to attend conferences has *helped me grow* as a professional. I also know that I have this option of saying "no" if I'm not interested. I'm "allowed" to make my own choices.

Conferences *challenge* me to grow in my profession. From such a conference I brought back ideas that were developed into a school-wide program. My feelings about this are positive because my efforts are supported, not coerced.

I was excited about being chosen to attend the Hands-On Science and Math Workshop. I know the principal valued my interest in becoming more proficient in science instruction and in instructing subject matter using the experimental hands-on approach. I have used all of the material our school received, and science instruction has been 90% hands-on/experimental approach. Her support *reinforces* my efforts.

In a few instances, pressure by principals to participate in workshops and other activities resulted in positive outcomes for teachers:

Now I am always *looking for new techniques* and technology to use for instruction in the math classroom as a result of my principal's encouragement to attend workshops. At times, the principal required attendance at workshops and required evidence that we were using the new techniques learned. At the time, I was irritated by her insistence to learn so many new things. As I look back, I really *gained a lot* from being pushed. I use my new knowledge frequently.

Unfortunately, some principals provided no instructional leadership beyond encouraging attendance at workshops. However, when workshops were a teacher's *only* opportunity to grow, teachers indicated that such workshops were worthwhile:

Workshops *tremendously influence* what I do in the classroom, especially because there is nothing else done at my school to give support. They introduce new teaching techniques and allow me to better plan for effective use of specific techniques.

Building a Culture of Collaboration and Learning

Studies of innovation show that sustained improvement in teaching often hinges on the development of "teachers as learners" who *collaborate* with one another to study teaching and its effects (rather than operate in isolation; see Lortie, 1975). This requires serious, ongoing *staff development*. Joyce and Showers (1995) write,

> Site-based "restructuring," "systemic" reform, and "quality man-agement" possess sufficient history now to enable us to recognize a disturbing prospect: Failure is in store for [these efforts] if they are not accompanied by extensive staff development of a strength and responsiveness that would be barely recognizable in the arrays of short courses provided 15 years ago. (pp. xiii-xiv)

In fact, our data point out that principals' leadership was frequently based on beliefs such as these:

- We are all *learners*; thus school is a "community of learners," including faculty, staff, students, parents, and administrators.
- We are all *lifelong* learners; thus, our goal is to prepare students for lifelong learning by teaching them (helping them learn) how to learn.
- We are all *coaches*; thus we learn from each other and help others learn.
- We are all colleagues and *collaborators*.
- We *openly discuss* our views and work toward consensus. This includes dialogue about curriculum, instruction, and program administration vis-à-vis students, teachers, administrators, supervisors, and parents. Such dialogue spans philosophy, belief, literature, and research. (See Figure 3.3 for an adaptation of Calhoun's [1994] matrix, which forms a basis for such discussions.)

In addition, the principals described in our study recognized that collaborative networks among educators are *essential* for successful teaching and learning and could be expanded through staff development. Meier (1995) states,

> Schools in which teachers are in frequent conversation with each other about their work, have easy and necessary access to each other's classrooms, and have the time to develop common standards for student performance are the ones that will succeed in developing new habits in students and their teachers. Teachers

	Parents	Teachers	Administrators and Supervisors	Community and Parents
Curriculum What should content be? What knowledge/ skills are of most worth?	1	2	3	4
Instruction How should the content be delivered? What instructional strategies should be used?	5	6	7	8
Administration How should the environment be managed?	9	10	11	12

Figure 3.3. Matrix for Discussion of Philosophies, Beliefs, Articles, Research, and Needs Among Groups

Adapted from *How to Use Action Research in the Self-Renewing School* (p. 115), by E. F. Calhoun, 1994, Alexandria, VA: Association for Supervision and Curriculum Development. Copyright © 1994 by ASCD. Adapted with permission. All rights reserved.

need frequent and easy give and take with professionals from allied fields—that is one mark of a true professional. They need opportunities to speak and write publicly about their work, attend conferences, read professional journals, and discuss something besides what they're going to do about Johnny on Monday. There must be some kind of combination of discomfiture and support—focused always on what does and does not have an impact on children's learning. (p. 143)

One common form of collaboration involved teachers sharing information and demonstrating skills to other teachers based on workshops and conferences they attended; this naturally assumes a high trust and comfort level among colleagues.

Why Is He or She Encouraging Collaboration?

Our data indicate that good principals encouraged collaboration to enhance teacher growth and development. This, in turn, enhanced their instructional performance, especially with regard to implementing *innovative ideas* and *solving student learning problems*:

> His goals are to build a faculty as a *collaborative team,* making decisions, and observing and encouraging each other to improve instruction.

Teachers also discussed staff development goals such as increasing harmony and ownership to support teachers' roles in *collaborative decision-making* processes:

> She is probably trying to improve teachers' *morale* and to promote *harmony* among teachers.

> Ed felt that if we as a staff could relate to each other on a more personal level, we would *care* more about each other. He hoped this would make our conversations more *open* and that our professional dialogue would be richer.

> I believe his goal is to give *ownership* of decision making to the teachers.

> [Having open meetings] is a subtle way of allowing us to *focus* on what we see as our concerns and to not impose an artificial agenda on us.

Strategies for Encouraging Collaboration

According to our study, good principals used several staff development strategies to encourage collaboration among teachers, as noted below.

1. Some principals encouraged schoolwide collaboration by consistently *modeling* a philosophy of teamwork.

> She tries to encourage a *team* effort among administrators, teachers, and students. She has a philosophy of discipline that allows

students to make choices, good or bad, and then have an opportunity to reflect upon their choices. This approach has carried over
into many areas of our school. Kids have choices, teachers have
choices, and in the classroom, kids are given more choices.

2. Principals supported the development of *formal* collaborative
structures among teachers through, for example, the use of *inter- and
intradepartmental and grade-level structures*:

> She set up *study groups* for people who were interested in learning
> new teaching strategies. In these groups we discussed ideas and
> frustrations.

Principals encouraged teacher-collaborative structures to work
together *regularly* on instructional issues:

> Our principal encourages our team to *meet* together regularly
> (bimonthly) to discuss our school's mathematics program. We
> discuss current status, individual student and staff needs, new
> programs (pros and cons), how to implement change if change is
> necessary and planning for parent/community involvement.

> Grade-level teams are strongly encouraged by the principal to
> *work together* on instructional strategies, problems, and pacing.
> The principal reviews the meeting minutes and offers helpful
> suggestions and praise.

> My principal encourages both myself and other members of my
> grade level by using our cooperative techniques as *examples* of
> appropriate working relationships in the school.

3. Good principals provided *planning time* as one major way to
encourage the development of formal instructional and curricular
collaboration among teachers. Sometimes approaches to providing
planning time were quite systematic:

> Our principal makes available *horizontal and vertical planning time*.
> Vertical planning occurs mainly during the summer. These are
> paid meeting times to discuss, review, and assess what has oc-
> curred and what should have occurred based on testing data,

teacher observation, and parent feedback—a very strong factor in our school. If any new programs are introduced, these kinds of sessions go on to introduce the expectations of each grade level to everyone. Horizontal planning time incorporates taking the essential elements and linking them to our text planning and innovations that are introduced to the curriculum.

My principal provides *release time* once a month for teams of grade-level teachers to meet to discuss concerns, make plans, and discuss new strategies to use in the classroom.

4. Some principals encouraged teachers to use *informal* collaborative arrangements. To illustrate, one principal created duty-free lunch periods to induce teachers to meet:

The principal has arranged for faculty members to have *duty-free* lunch time daily, and once a month refreshments are provided by teachers for the faculty during morning or afternoon *break time.* These short get-together time periods enable teachers a chance to visit with each other and escape the routine of classroom duties . . . it's a way of warding off burnout for teachers . . . it helps us share ideas and relate with others.

To enhance staff development, principals also advocated the use of *cooperative teaching, informal "rethinking,"* and *sharing* among teachers to explore instructional problems and issues:

He encouraged me to *share* my ideas with regular education teachers so as to support instruction and discipline throughout the school.

In some cases, principals provided opportunities for informal collaboration among teachers working on *special projects.*

She *allows me,* with the help of other teachers, *to create* a curriculum map. This map shows what we want to teach at certain parts of the school year. We list topics and subtopics, and she generally approves what we plan to teach the next year.

Sometimes, principals supported *impromptu* collaborative efforts:

Whenever I go to the principal for advice about a behavior problem that I'm dealing with, he always compliments me on my methods, reminds me I've done well with problems in the past, and reassures me that we'll get through it. He usually pulls the child's file, reviews with me recent dealings with the student, and offers to call in a *problem-solving team* with other staff members.

A few teachers reported that *principals participated* in informal cooperative planning to encourage faculty collaboration.

She *joins our* team during team planning . . . she informally drops in. As a result she is accessible when we have ideas about new activities, strategies, etc. that we would like to try.

5. Principals also requested that *teachers observe one another* in their classrooms as a form of collaboration. (This is discussed further in the section on *coaching*.)

Our principal *encourages peer observation* and reflection. It was valuable to talk about teaching with someone going through the same thing I was—the peer teacher was great.

The most effective strategy my principal employs is to encourage the faculty to *observe each other* with particular methodologies in mind. For instance, when I was having difficulty in building for transfer during closure, he encouraged me to observe a colleague who was particularly effective in that area. On the other hand, because I am strong with transitions, he sent a teacher to observe my practice.

The Effects of Collaboration on Developing Faculty

The myriad formal and informal opportunities principals provided for teacher collaboration yielded vast positive results for teachers. The following quotes are illustrative of the many enthusiastic comments we found in our data about collaboration. They show major impacts on teachers' motivation, self-esteem, confidence, and ownership of decisions. Also apparent were strong impacts on teacher reflection and reflectively informed instructional behavior (e.g., instructional variety, risk taking, focus, discretion) and, of course, teacher-teacher collaborative interaction itself:

> By observing other teachers, I have been able to think of my own teaching strengths and weaknesses from a *new perspective.* I have become *more willing to ask for help* from my principal and fellow teachers. We have all become *more open to admitting difficulties* and asking for help rather than closing ourselves off and complaining. I am very *happy* to be valued in that environment.

> Working with other teachers influences me to *think* about my teaching in relation to theirs, and it influences me *to use techniques* that other teachers are using. Collaboration influences teachers *to come out of their world* to see what others are doing. Teachers need help to "break the mold."

> Collaborative practices establish the idea that teachers are the knowledge source. Peer interaction has more impact than outside assistance. My own *confidence* levels have increased as I have been developing in an environment in which practice and application are encouraged and assistance is provided through both colleagues and supervisors. Teachers *feel free* to explore new options, share, and learn from both success and failure. I feel *appreciated* and *motivated* each day to continue to grow and learn from peers.

> I readily participate in collaborative planning. I have access to the Instructional Committee and can impact procedural policy. I feel that my *opinion is valued.* I regularly *seek out informal conversations* and attend meetings to voice my concerns and hear those of others.

> Planning together has made me more *aware* of appropriate instructional strategies and more aware of the overall picture in the school—beyond discussions with K-5 teachers. I am also more *focused* on different levels within my class because of the ideas and input I have heard from others.

> Working as a team to plan, implement, and evaluate instruction provided me with new strategies and ideas and the *confidence* that my plans were meeting student needs and school goals. I was

motivated to "stay on target" with the agreed-upon plans and pacing. I was *focused* on working with my team to provide the best instructional program to students.

It is *motivating* to work with a leader who shows great confidence in our abilities and is so encouraging of taking risks (try new things, change). I take more *risks,* try *new* programs and teaching strategies, and work toward inclusion and integration. I have a great deal of latitude in how to achieve these goals.

I became *reflective* of my teaching behaviors and schoolwide discipline policy. A schoolwide disciplinary committee was formed, and a schoolwide program was developed and implemented.

I stretched out and *tried* new strategies because of the support the team provided. I *liked my job* more. I liked the staff and kids more because we *supported each other* and were responsible for each other. I became a better teacher, I *worked harder* to find solutions, and I was *anxious to share* whatever I learned with other members of our team. Our conversations were more *open* and our professional dialogue became *richer.*

Collaboration allows teachers to *focus* on what we see as our concerns and to not have an artificial agenda imposed on us.

I feel more that I have decision-making power as a teacher. This helps me have an *investment in decision making.* I believe I *work harder* with instructional strategies that I've had a hand in deciding.

I have become more concerned with *giving the students a "voice."* Teachers feel much better with choices, and I hope the kids do also. It's now more of a *team effort* between the administrator, teacher, and student. Everyone has become an active participant in learning and a better decision maker.

Although collaboration resulted in overwhelmingly positive effects, some teachers qualified their remarks. They pointed to occasional problems such as the issue of responsibility, lack of time, overload, a principal's habit of vetoing teachers' collaborative decisions, and the use of teacher collaboration by principals as a way to avoid decision making:

> Well, collaboration is great when things are going well, but when they are not, a peer is put in a tough situation. If the principal is not directly involved, who is *responsible*?

> Collaboration promotes a spirit of cooperation and commitment. When what the group has decided is *not* implemented, when these ideas are discarded by the principal—without much consideration and with little or no explanation—it *deflates* the group enthusiasm.

> I like the idea of creating curriculum maps with my colleagues. I dislike when she [the principal] *"strikes out"* something everyone wants to do and worked so hard on.

> Collaborative opportunities are excellent; however, it is an ongoing process and takes time for everyone to understand and accept. It is more work, also. Everyone has to take more *responsibility*.

Promoting Coaching: A New Dimension of Staff Development

Insights From the Research

From analyses of studies conducted between the 1960s and 1980s, Joyce and Showers (1983) reached a powerful conclusion: Classroom implementation of the training design was far more effective if the training included *coaching* from a peer at the classroom level and if it occurred after presentation of theory, demonstration, and practice of a skill:

> Peer coaching . . . is the collaborative work of teachers to solve the problems/questions that arise during implementation; it begins in training settings and continues in the workplace following initial training. Peer coaching provides both support for the community of teachers attempting to master new skills and the time for planning and lesson development so essential to changes in curriculum and instruction. (Joyce & Showers, 1995, p. 110)

These researchers explained that coaching contributes to the transfer of training in five ways:

1. Coached teachers generally *practiced new strategies more frequently and developed greater skill in the actual moves* of a new teaching strategy than did uncoached teachers who had experienced identical initial training. In fact, the horizontal transfer (i.e., the making of adjustments so a teaching strategy better fits a specific context and set of students) so necessary for bringing an innovation learned in staff development sessions to the classroom occurs only when teachers are coached.

2. Coached teachers *used their newly learned strategies more appropriately* than uncoached teachers in terms of their own instructional objectives and the theories of specific models of teaching.

3. Coached teachers *exhibited greater long-term retention of knowledge about and skill with strategies* in which they had been coached and, as a group, increased the appropriateness of use of new teaching models over time.

4. Coached teachers were much more likely than uncoached teachers to *teach new models of teaching to their students,* ensuring that students understood the purpose of the strategy and the behaviors expected of them when using the strategy.

5. Coached teachers *exhibited clearer cognition with regard to the purposes and uses of the new strategies,* as revealed through interviews, lesson plans, and classroom performance than did uncoached teachers. (Joyce & Showers, 1995, pp. 119-120, emphasis ours)

Joyce and Showers (1995) also discovered that the level of implementation of an instructional innovation can reach 90% to 100% when whole-school faculties are organized into peer-coaching teams for follow-up to training. (For details about a variation of coaching for reflection, cognitive coaching, see Chapter 4).

Our Findings About Coaching as an Element of Staff Development

We found substantial evidence that good principals advocated coaching among teachers for purposes of teacher development.

1. *Teacher as Model.* Principals encouraged teachers to model for each other to (1) improve teaching and (2) motivate and recognize exemplary teachers:

> Teachers are exposed to new options and ideas and can *learn from* the successes and failures of *other teachers.*

> He wants me to feel like my work is *worth it*, to get me *more involved* with other teachers so we will do more of the same.

Specifically, principals actively encouraged teachers to *visit the classrooms* of exemplary teachers, asked exemplary teachers to serve as *models* to other teachers, and encouraged teachers to make *presentations* within their school and district and at professional conferences:

> My principal invites other teachers to *observe* my teaching after discussing it with me. Though I seldom hear directly that he likes what I'm doing, it makes me feel good that he uses my teaching techniques as examples to share with other people; therefore he must like what I'm doing. He sends promising interview candidates to observe me as well as older and tenured teachers who are on remediation.

> She uses activities and lessons I do *as examples* of good planning and good teaching. She asks me to share ideas with other teachers and to mentor new teachers.

> Our principal often *notes* strategies of teachers that are very effective. She encourages teachers to reflect on such strengths, and she then motivates them toward *presenting* the ideas and strategies to the other faculty members. Several teachers have presented staff development workshops.

I was encouraged to *teach* a thematic unit in the kaleidoscope seminar for K-1st grade teachers at a *statewide conference.* My principal encouraged me to take some of the things I was using in my classroom and present them. I wrote a presentation to share with 30 to 40 people for two sessions.

He uses me as an *example* of instructional empowerment and change, versus stagnation.

Teachers found that modeling good teaching for their colleagues led to greater *confidence, motivation,* and *self-esteem.* Modeling for colleagues also increased a teacher's own *reflection* and *reflectively informed* behavior:

He encourages me to share my teaching techniques with others; it makes me *think* that what I'm doing is working. Having another pair of eyes in my room, whether it be student teachers, recruits, or tenured teachers, makes me *want to improve* my teaching and be at my best. It makes me *feel good* about myself. But . . . I have to wonder if the teachers (particularly the tenured) don't resent the fact that the principal requires them to come see me.

She asks me to share my ideas with other teachers and to mentor new teachers. I think of myself as an effective teacher whose work is *appreciated* by my principal. I look for *new innovative methods* of teaching language arts skills—ones that require the use of higher order thinking skills.

I was encouraged to teach a unit at a seminar at the university. I was nervous because I had never presented before a big group. I was *flattered* that she thought my ideas were good enough to present. This encouraged me to believe in my abilities more, and I was more *enthusiastic* and *inspired* to do more in my classroom.

He sent teachers to observe my classrooms. This made me *feel good* about myself and my teaching and also inspired me to look for ways to stay on top of current topics. I was more *confident* when I went into the classroom. It caused me to think about what I did well and figure out what can be done better.

2. *Teacher as Learner.* For purposes of professional growth, good principals encouraged teachers to *visit* other schools to observe classrooms and programs:

> My principal encourages us to *visit* other schools to get new ideas about teaching strategies and lets me make the decision about implementing these ideas.

> My principal encourages me to push further or find out more about a topic. When developmental math first became a "topic," the school mandated its implementation. I was not impressed and was vocal about my feelings. She encouraged me to *visit* schools where successful implementation was occurring. I was better able to make an informed decision about this topic, and I was free to use my own judgment in how I implemented the mandated strategies.

Unfortunately, in most cases, teachers indicated that principals could not provide the kind of support (e.g., providing substitutes) for visits to other schools, thus limiting the occurrence of such visits.

Observing in other classrooms had positive effects on teacher *self-esteem* and *risk taking*; it also yielded greater *reflection* and reflectively informed behavior in the classroom:

> Visiting other schools helped me keep an *open mind* when approaching new topics. I have felt *validated* as a professional by my principal. It has encouraged me to develop as a *risk taker.* I have been better able to make decisions about curriculum, and I feel free to use professional judgment in how I implement new strategies.

> This strategy makes me feel more like a *professional* and helps me to improve my teaching. I have changed some of my teaching strategies as I *implement new ideas.* The technique is nonthreatening, and I am allowed to make decisions about the changes myself.

Using Inquiry to Drive Staff Development

An essential part of staff development is training in collection and analysis of data about student learning. Without class- and school-based data about learning and the impact of implementing new strategies on student learning, teachers *cannot properly determine* the effects of what they and others do in the classroom (Calhoun, 1994). The good principals described by teachers in our study operated staff development as a large-scale action research project (despite the fact that they largely failed to use action research to the degree they knew was necessary). One teacher noted,

> The principal uses *surveys* to determine our needs and our educational background. Then we plan inservices to meet needs as indicated by the survey results.

For a basic understanding of action research, we recommend Calhoun's *How to Use Action Research in the Self-Renewing School* (1994). This highly useful guide to action research is based on work with educators throughout the world. Among other things, Calhoun describes the phases of effective action research:

1. Selecting an area or focus
2. Collecting data
3. Organizing data
4. Analyzing and interpreting data (and prior to Step 5: Studying the professional literature)
5. Taking action
6. Repeat Steps 1-5 again and again

She notes,

> The quest for school renewal through action research . . .
> - is a route to immediate student *outcomes*;
> - can develop the school as a *learning community*;
> - can build organizational capacity to *solve problems*;
> - is a staff development program through the study of *literature* and on-site *data* and the determination of optimum *actions* for implementation; and
> - can be *personal* and *professional* development. (Calhoun, 1994, p. 100)

Calhoun (1994) also discusses the problem-solving potential of action research:

By centering action on the careful collection of data to diagnose problems, a disciplined search for alternative solutions, an agreement to act, and the conscientious monitoring of whether and how much the solution worked—with a recycling of the process, either attacking the problem again or focusing on another one—we live the problem-solving process for ourselves and model it for our students. The potential is the development of a professional ethos in which members of the organization continually strive to improve their performance by learning to solve more and more problems. (p. 8)

PSSSSST! Redesign

In his recent pamphlet, Villars (1991) describes the "mindless periodicity" and rigid increments of time that characterize most schools. Villars eloquently makes the case for nurturing student talent, encouraging self-directed and cooperative learning, and developing student self-worth and creativity through a multitude of diverse approaches to teaching and learning. He contends that open spaces, a variety of learning options, differentiated roles for staff, and flexible learning time are examples of ways to achieve educational goals. *In fact, our study data strongly confirm the importance of these elements to enhancing teacher development, fostering reflective teaching, and improving student learning.* Specifically, Villars suggests that to achieve optimal learning, we consider redesigning the following elements (known as PSSSST) of schooling:

- **Purposes** (varies with individual)
- **Students** (grouping, continuous progress)
- **Strategies** (for teaching and learning)
- **Stuff** (materials and resources used)
- **Staff** (differentiated personnel and assignments)
- **Space** (including rooms, study areas, libraries, other sites)
- **Time** (flexible amounts)

Providing Resources to Support Growth and Improvement

The teachers we studied explained that good principals helped to develop faculty by providing essential resources and that this greatly enhanced teacher growth, classroom teaching, and student learning:

> I believe she gets a kick out of *helping* people realize their potential. This also created a school filled with people recognized throughout the county.

> He encourages instruction that meets the *needs* of students.

According to our data, principals provided resources, sometimes in liberal amounts, to support teacher growth and improved classroom instruction:

> She will let our teachers buy *anything* within reason that is necessary for teaching effectively. She openly states instruction of students is our chief priority, and any resource we might need to that end gets first priority.

Classroom materials were the most frequently described available resource (e.g., supplies; subject-matter texts including books and printed matter; manipulatives, games, and kits). Occasionally, principals gave teachers small amounts of money ($100 to $200) to purchase classroom materials. Several teachers reported that principals also provided them with parent volunteers and paraprofessionals.

> She does what she can to *provide* necessary instructional resources. Our school has a form that teachers can fill out listing the resources they need. The form goes to our teacher council. The teacher has a representative present a rationale for the need. Most often the request is approved and the material is bought immediately.

> She is constantly *asking* us what resources she can find for us to improve our current teaching or classroom.

> She offers *stipends* for classes taken to improve classroom performance.

> She encourages parent *volunteers* to come into the classroom and participate in various instructional areas (for example, planning, games, and reading with children).

Our study produced no evidence that the availability of resources strongly affected teachers' feelings; however, having resources did yield major impacts on teacher *reflection* and *reflectively informed behavior*:

I enjoy teaching with the materials provided. My instructional strategies have improved because I have the requisite materials. It *motivates* me.

Extra classroom materials help me be *creative* in our lesson plans. I came up with different activities that students could work on. The extra money allows individual teachers the *freedom* to buy materials as they see fit.

I am more *willing* to try more various activities that might be considered a little extreme, but knowing I have her support, I know I can make it work for the kids. I really don't mind taking some chances because of our support base.

Her help [in providing resources] *encouraged* me to be *reflective,* be on the cutting edge, and be a risk taker. She encouraged me to jump in. If I messed up, I would say oops and try again! I felt safe. Her emphases were always on personal growth and professionalism. My achievements were her achievements. She was not threatened by my success; she enjoyed it.

Tips for Leaders

Based on the collective reports of teachers who participated in our study, we suggest that principals consider the following to enhance professional development:

1. Building an atmosphere and processes of *democracy* (shared decision making and collective responsibility) and a *culture of learning* among teachers and administrators.

2. Learning, with the faculty and parents, about *school improvement* and staff development.

3. Providing training in *action research*.

4. Collectively assessing the *effects* of instruction and the climate of the school.

5. Organizing a staff development *council* to coordinate activities (see Wolf, 1994, for guidelines and resources).

6. Focusing staff development programs on the areas of *curriculum, instruction*, and *technology,* as they are more likely to have effects on student learning.

7. Organizing *study groups* and supporting their activities.

8. Developing *peer coaching* relationships and supporting their activities. (See Joyce & Showers, 1995, and Showers & Joyce, 1996, for more detail on Nos. 7 and 8, study groups and peer coaching.)

9. Providing time for collaboration for the *study of teaching and learning*. This will reduce the isolation, not the autonomy, that alienates teachers from each other.

10. Encouraging a *commitment* to spend time studying outcomes, curriculum, and teaching practice rather than administrivia and technical or managerial matters. Put differently, increase time spent on items toward the top of the list below, and decrease time spent on items at the bottom (many educators have this backwards!):

More
Outcomes
Curriculum
Instruction
Technology
Daily concerns/technical matters
Enrichment/gimmicks
Less

11. Providing time for *study* of implementation of *innovations* in curriculum, teaching, and instruction.

12. Encouraging individual teachers to develop instructional *goals* and *objectives* and to meet with teachers to discuss their progress. Two teachers in our study noted:

> My principal has me select a personal *goal* that will help me grow professionally. He then checks on my goal midway through the year and at the end of the year. His goal is to help push me into something that will help me grow professionally.

> About 6 years ago, our principal initiated an evaluation process whereby each certified staff member wrote up professional and instructional *goals* for himself/herself for the next 3-year period. He then discussed these goals with me at my yearly evaluation. Goals stressed stepping out and trying something new. Each year progress toward the goals was discussed and new goals were set. The district curriculum and instruction coordinator worked with the principals and teachers to set up inservices and summer courses that would help teachers reach their identified goals. The atmosphere of professional acceptance and support was also enhanced by occasional visits to the classroom. Each time a hand-written message was left for students and teacher about the learning that was taking place.

Summary

In this chapter we have described, often in the words of teachers' themselves, effective approaches to staff development used by instructional leaders. Our findings about staff development programs in action are consistent with those of related research about the importance of professional growth for teachers. Darling-Hammond and McLaughlin (1995), for example, suggest that staff development

- Involves teachers in the acts of teaching, assessing, observing, and reflecting that lead to understanding of learning and development

- Responds to needs of participants as revealed through inquiry, reflection, and experimentation
- Focuses on collaborative communities of practitioners
- Relates to real work with real students
- Sustains and supports participants through collaborative problem solving
- Connects to school improvement (p. 598)

The fundamental challenge for educational leaders, then, is one of building a culture of lifelong learning through inquiry and collaboration.

Reflection:
Encouraging Critical Study

> [*Reflective thinking*] *involves (1) a state of doubt, hesita-*
> *tion, perplexity, mental difficulty, in which thinking origi-*
> *nates, and (2) an act of searching, hunting, inquiring, to*
> *find material that will resolve the doubt, settle and dispose*
> *of the perplexity.*

> Dewey, 1933, p. 12

In recent years, the process of *reflective practice* has been acknowledged as a potentially powerful enhancement to supervisor-teacher
interaction. In fact, researchers now believe that the experience of
reflection may be a very potent factor in increasing the *complexity of
teachers' thinking about teaching-learning problems* in the same way it has
been shown to be potent in enhancing the problem-solving skills of
experts (Frederiksen, 1984). Our research bears this out.

This chapter begins with a discussion of the notion of and the need
for reflective practice. We also review related research, the development of reflective thinking frameworks, and different approaches to
reflective instructional leadership. We then discuss our findings: the
characteristics of teacher reflection, the primary principal behaviors
identified in our study that foster reflective practice, and the benefits

of reflective practice for teachers. Last, we discuss cognitive coaching as a bridge to reflection and present tips for principals working to encourage teacher reflection.

The Need for Reflective Practice

The act of teaching is demanding and complex because teachers' knowledge is necessarily contextual, interactive, nonroutine, and speculative. Teachers' work, by nature, requires the following:

- Opportunities to *reframe the experiences* of teaching in previously unheard of or unthought of ways
- Development of *problem-solving skills*, new thinking patterns, and alternative perspectives
- Generation of myriad *alternatives*
- *Hypothesis building* based on knowledge
- *Assessment of actions* so as to create new learnings (Clark & Lampert, 1986)

However, professionals in general—and teachers in particular—seldom receive the kind of meaningful feedback that leads to professional development (Bridges, 1986; McGregor, 1960).

Reflective practice is founded on the assumption that increased awareness of one's professional performance can result in considerable improvement of performance. Specifically, reflection on teaching has been advocated by many as a means to question teaching/learning events in order to bring one's teaching actions to a conscious level, to interpret the consequences of one's actions, and to conceptualize alternative teaching actions (Clark & Lampert, 1986; Colton & Sparks-Langer, 1993; Lewis & Dowling, 1992; Meyer, 1992; Ross & Hannay, 1986). Osterman (1990) identifies these purposes of reflection:

- Greater self-awareness
- Development of new knowledge about professional practice
- A broader understanding of problems confronting practitioners

Schön (1987) describes the practitioner who is engaged in reflection as a *builder of repertoire* through inquiry, rather than a collector of procedures and methods. The practice of reflection provides new insight into the meaning of teaching events; it is also a vehicle for developing *metateaching skills,* that is, the ability to think about the thinking of teaching (Marchant, 1989).

An environment that encourages risk taking, inquiry, and critical thinking is considered essential to the growth of teachers as reflective professionals (Ross & Hannay, 1986). Educational scholars have concluded that such growth requires an environment that fosters efficacy (the belief that desired results are attainable), flexibility (the ability to accommodate others' viewpoints and to adapt to changing circumstances), social responsibility (the understanding that knowledge is not gained in isolation but rather through active participation and discussion with colleagues), and consciousness (a willingness to consider multiple factors influencing cognitive processes of decision making) (Colton & Sparks-Langer, 1993). Indeed, reflective practice is empowering: Through communication and collaboration, individuals become "more effective, . . . assume greater responsibility for their own performance, and . . . engage more closely and more productively with others in the workplace" (Osterman & Kottkamp, 1993, p. 185).

Principals can provide many of the critical elements that support reflective practice: rich opportunities for interaction, shared reflection, and modeling for reflective practice (Grimmett, 1988). They can engage teachers in a learning process that is challenging and rewarding, a process founded on beliefs that comprise a *credo* for reflective practice. Clearly, the effective principals in our study used strategies—for example, giving descriptive feedback, asking questions, soliciting feedback and opinions, and listening actively in conferences—that researchers have linked to the development of teacher reflection (Osterman & Kottkamp, 1993). (See Bolton, 1979, for an in-depth discussion of communication skills that are essential to reflective practice.) Regarding reflection, Osterman and Kottkamp (1993) wrote:

1. Everyone needs professional growth opportunities.
2. All professionals want to improve.
3. All professionals can learn.
4. All professionals are capable of assuming responsibility for their own professional growth and development.

5. People need and want information about their own performance.
6. Collaboration enriches professional development. (pp. 46-47)

Eltis and Turney (1992), Feiman-Nemser (1990), and Schön (1983, 1987) have argued that reflection should be a standard professional disposition, a view with which we strongly agree. Hatton and Smith (1995) drew on Dewey's (1933) original concept of reflection—which itself derives from the thinking of such educators as Plato, Aristotle, Confucius, and Buddha, as demonstrated by Houston (1988)—to define reflection as "deliberate thinking about action with a view to its improvement" (p. 40). Accordingly, a complete cycle of professional "doing"—coupled with reflection—yields modified action (Grant & Zeichner, 1984). Such action can be contrasted with *routine action*, which is derived from impulse, tradition, and authority (Hatton & Smith, 1995). Put simply, reflection involves a cycle of (1) recognizing doubt or *uncertainty*, (2) drawing *inferences* based on previous experiences, (3) choosing a course of action, and (4) *testing* inferences and choices through further reflection (Grimmett & Erickson, 1988; Schön, 1983).

Related Research and the Development of Frameworks for Reflective Thinking

Through a process of ongoing study and debate, Hatton and Smith (1995) developed an operational framework (derived from F. Fuller, 1970; Smith & Hatton, 1993; and Valli, 1992) that identifies a developmental sequence of five levels of reflection and the specific nature of those levels. Broadly speaking, Level 1 is identified as "technical rationality," or reflection that addresses self and task concerns. Levels 2, 3, and 4 are referred to as descriptive, dialogic, and critical reflection, respectively; they constitute "reflection-on-action," which deals with task and impact concerns. Level 5, or "reflection-in-action" (contextualization), centers on the impacts of behavior after experience in a profession.

Alrichter and Posch (1989) and Gilson (1989) describe reflection-in-action, the highest level, as part of the artistry (or intuitive knowledge) gained through professional experience: This includes engaging in a reflective conversation with oneself, shaping situations with respect to one's frame of reference, and reframing using holistic (more contextual) interpretations. These five levels include the relatively simple as well as the more complex, sustained, insightful, and multi-dimensional; as such, they permit professionals to become increasingly aware of the impact of their actions on clients (e.g., students; Smith & Hatton, 1993).

More specifically, Hatton and Smith's (1995) developmental operational framework is described in terms of the following:

1. *Technical reflection* (decision making about immediate behaviors and skills), drawn from a research/theory base
2. *Descriptive reflection* (analyzing one's social efficiency, development, personal growth), seeking "best practice"
3. *Dialogic reflection* (deliberative, cognitive, narrative), weighing competing viewpoints and exploring alternatives
4. *Critical reflection* (social reconstructionist), seeing goals and practices as problematic according to ethical criteria
5. *Contextualization of multiple viewpoints*, applying Levels 1-4 above to situations as they are taking place

A similar hierarchy of reflection was proposed by van Manen (1977), who derived three levels from Habermas's (1968/1978) work: technical reflection, which is concerned with efficiency and effectiveness; practical reflection, including examination of one's goals and one's means; and critical reflection, which adds consideration of moral and ethical criteria as well as sociohistorical and political-cultural contexts to the first two levels (Sparks-Langer & Colton, 1991; Valli, 1992; van Manen, 1977). Regarding the latter, Smyth (1989) argues that teachers should be concerned with questions of equity and justice in classroom teaching. See Figure 4.1 for a summary of reflective thinking levels according to various investigators.

We used Eastern Michigan University's CITE (Collaboration for the Improvement of Teacher Education) framework, which is consistent with current theories, to assess data about teachers' reflective thinking produced by our study. This framework, which is based on Gagne's (1968) hierarchy of thinking as well as van Manen's (1977) concept of critical reflection, has seven levels, as described by Sparks-Langer and Colton (1991):

Investigator	R-Level 1	R-Level 2	R-Level 3	R-Level 4
Hatton & Smith, 1995	*Technical Rationality.* Self and task concerns: making decisions about immediate behaviors or skills by applying new information drawn from theory or research	*Descriptive Reflection.* Analyzing social efficiency, development, and personal growth factors and seeking "best practice"	*Dialogic Reflection.* Deliberate cognitive narrative, weighing different viewpoints, and exploring alternatives	*Critical Reflection.* Considering goals and practices as problematic according to ethical criteria
Alrichter & Posch, 1989; Gilson, 1989				
van Manen, 1977	*Technical Reflection.* Concern with efficiency and effectiveness	*Practical Reflection.* Examination of personal goals and the means to goal attainment		*Critical Reflection.* Consideration of moral and ethical criteria, socio-historical context, and political-cultural contexts
Sparks-Langer & Colton, 1991	No description of teaching-learning events	Simple description of teaching-learning events	Labeling of events with pedagogical concepts	Explanation using only tradition or personal preference

Figure 4.1. Reflective Thinking Levels

Investigator	R-Level 5	R-Level 6	R-Level 7
Hatton & Smith, 1995	*Contextual.* Applying Levels 1-4 to new situations while the activity unfolds		
Alrichter & Posch, 1989; Gilson, 1989	**Artistry and/or intuitive** knowledge that develops from experience; conversation with self and reframing		
van Manen, 1977			
Sparks-Langer & Colton, 1991	Explanation using pedagogical principles	Explanation using pedagogical principles and context	Explanation with moral/ethical considerations

Figure 4.1. Reflective Thinking Levels, continued

1. *No description* of teaching behaviors
2. *Simple description* of teaching behaviors
3. Labeling of teaching/learning events using *pedagogical* concepts
4. *Explanation* of teaching behaviors using only *tradition or personal preference*
5. *Explanation* of teaching behaviors using *pedagogical principles*
6. *Explanation* of teaching behaviors using *pedagogical principles* and context
7. *Explanation* of teaching behaviors using *ethical/moral considerations* (Sparks-Langer & Colton, 1991, p. 39)

The good principals described in our study encouraged reflective conversations with teachers at all levels (see Figure 4.2 for samples of such talk, by reflective levels). In particular, one can see the increasing contextualization and multifaceted critique implied in examples of talk at higher reflection levels.

Approaches to Reflective Supervision

Several approaches to what we call "reflective supervision" (wherein the principal supports, encourages, and guides reflective teaching) are described by Pajak (1993). He suggests that the primary *emphases* of all these approaches are (1) *professional* knowledge (Schön, 1988), (2) *social* reconstruction (Zeichner & Liston 1987), (3) *historical* embeddedness (Garman, 1990), (4) *political* justice (Retallick, 1990; Smyth, 1990), and (5) *cultural* responsiveness (Bowers & Flinders, 1991). In other words, understanding teaching and learning must be placed in the context of students' and schools' social, historical, political, and cultural considerations.

The most common emphases of the good principals described in our research were professional knowledge and social reconstruction. In essence, principals provoked in teachers the ability to notice odd and unexpected things, frame a puzzle or question from them, become curious, inquire and explore, and be willing to adjust student learning experiences accordingly (see Schön, 1988, for more details). However, we also learned that good principals seldom encouraged teacher reflection in terms of historical, political, and cultural considerations.

Reflective Thinking Levels	Examples From Our Data
1. No description of teacher-learning events	1. No description
2. Simple, layperson description of teaching learning events	2. "I decided to move the reference books so the students could reach them more easily."
3. Labeling of events with pedagogical concepts	3. "Every time I teach, I state the objective of the lesson."
4. Explanation using only tradition or personal preference as rationale	4. "I kept the setup the same as the previous teacher had it. She said it helped control the class."
5. Explanation using pedagogical principles (principle or theory) as rationale	5. "Every day we review the previous learning and reinforce it so that students will retain the learning."
6. Explanation using pedagogical principles *and* context (student, personnel, community factors)	6. "These are Hispanic students, so I address their problems with English by providing more wait time."
7. Explanation with moral, ethical, political considerations	7. "I gave him money to use the library copier out of my own pocket because otherwise his learning would have been affected by his economic situation. Next time, I will restrict *all* students to use books and journals only."

Figure 4.2. Reflective Thinking Levels Adapted From CITE (Sparks-Langer, Simmons, Pasch, Colton, & Starko, 1990) and Illustrated by Teacher Talk

(More on our findings about the principal's role in facilitating teacher reflection is presented later in this chapter.)

Our Study: Characteristics of Teacher Reflection

Teachers, students, and even administrators should be learners. Yet, the typical milieu of the school makes it difficult for teachers to see themselves as learners, to reflect on practice, and to create a collaborative, intellectual environment that sustains them as a community of learners. Despite this, we know that the kind of social interaction necessary for teacher learning and growth can be promoted, in part, by instructional leaders who value dialogue that encourages teachers to become aware of and critically reflect on their learning and professional practice.

Although we cannot determine precisely what conditions of work and what kinds of interactions foster teacher reflection, nor what patterns comprise the basic nature of teacher reflection, we have found in our study, as others have found, that principals who are successful instructional leaders, at minimum, behaved in ways consistent with the following points:

1. A reflective orientation includes a tendency to analyze situations, to question what is happening and why it is happening, to identify what student learning is desired, and to have a sense of self-efficacy (J. J. Fuller & Brown, 1975). The leader's responsibility is akin to coaching, modeling, and collaborative dialogue (Pugach, 1990).

2. Reflective thinking levels increase after coaching (Pasch, Arpin, Kragt, Garcia, & Harberts, 1990).

3. Basic coaching involves describing, informing, confronting, and restructuring (Smyth, 1989). For example, the following questions may be posed by the principal:

    a. What did you plan to do in the lesson?
    b. Why did you approach it that way?
    c. What happened during the lesson?
    d. What does that mean to you?
    e. How might you do things differently?

4. The focus of reflection may be the teacher's thoughts *about previous action* and/or the teacher's thought processes that occurred *during (in) action* (Grant & Zeichner, 1984).

5. Reflection may take hold immediately or in a more extended and systematic time frame (Schön, 1983).

6. Reflection may be problem centered or focused on historical, cultural, and political values or beliefs as they relate to practical problems (Gore & Zeichner, 1991).

7. Although teachers may enhance reflection through journal writing and documentation of their learning, many report a preference for oral rather than written tasks as they learn to reflect on their work, as well as a preference for working with others (a peer or a supervisor) (Cutler, Cook, & Young, 1989).

8. Reflective practice helps teachers, as professionals, to express themselves or to "find their voice" (Freidus, 1991).

Principal Behaviors Fostering Reflection in Teachers and the Benefits to Teachers

Our study provided compelling evidence of the dramatic effects of principals' behaviors on the reflective capacities of teachers. These behaviors include modeling, classroom observation, dialogue, suggestion, and praise.

Modeling. Powerful effects on teachers' thinking and behavior resulted from seeing principals model good teaching. For instance, after watching her principal teach a complicated concept to students, a teacher commented:

> *Now* when I create lesson plans, I think in terms of how to make a concept understandable to a teenager. I understand that I should present material in digestible parts. I also tend not to get annoyed if a student misses something; instead, I redirect my method of instruction.

Classroom Observation. Simple classroom observation (even without dialogue or feedback) by principals encouraged teachers to reflect on their teaching and to make behavioral changes:

> My principal's visits make me feel that I'm seen as a valuable individual. I'm more motivated to teach better and to investigate better ways of teaching. His visits encourage me to *get input* from others and to *have an open mind.*

Dialogue With Teachers. Most important, the dialogue (which frequently includes encouragement, feedback, and questioning about instruction) between a principal and a teacher during formal conferences (usually based on classroom observation) enhanced teacher *reflection* about teaching methods and expected student outcomes, as well as informed teachers' classroom behavior. The following quotes illustrate this sharpened reflection:

> A lot of times when we teach, we do things but forget the meanings of them and why we do them. This [talking] reinforces the *meaning.*

> Reflection allows you to *think about* and to evaluate your strategies.

> I take more time to *think about* how I can best implement my talents. I think each day of more than one way to improve in each subject area. She knows that using my talents is better. Her approach encourages critical thinking throughout the building.

> I already know what I'm doing with my students, but the specific feedback does cause me to *examine* my actions and techniques more carefully. He made me realize that I make a difference. He cared enough to notice.

> I am constantly *thinking,* What can I do to improve? What are my weaknesses? What changes in my classroom will help?

> I don't feel threatened; he knows I'm a good teacher. When we talked about wait time, he phrased it positively: "You ask wonderful, thought-provoking questions. Should you give kids longer

to think about answers?" I knew it was true, so I *paid attention* and improved.

Her encouragement and tolerance for my attempts at improving instruction made me more *aware* of my own tolerance level for my students' attempts at learning. It made me realize that I should not stifle students' attempts to question traditional beliefs. Her encouragement made me want to succeed for the benefit of the students.

Increasing my *knowledge base* in methods of instruction gives me the background to feel secure in trying new methods.

Feedback makes me *think* deeper. It makes me get more information and collect more concrete data needed for instructional decisions.

She makes me feel more positive so I can *think* things through better and act more reasonable; I don't act on impulses. I stop and do what is right and in the best interests of the child.

Suggestion. Suggestions by principals often increased teacher reflection, especially creativity (particularly when principals conveyed a healthy respect for experimentation and used a nonthreatening approach), *and* increased teachers' reflectively informed behavior:

My principal's goal is to encourage us to be interesting and creative in the classroom. He makes me feel like it's OK to make mistakes, and I don't feel like I've failed because something wasn't spectacular. I do more *creative* things, and I have my students do more creative application problems like building models, writing math stories, and creating board games using math.

He caused me to examine many avenues of lesson delivery. Now I *teach from all domains* and for all learning styles.

Her suggestions encouraged me to continually be *reflective* about my teaching and student responses/outcomes. As I am teaching, I am more conscious of student attention, understanding, and independent work. I am not afraid to change my strategies or desired outcomes based on the feedback I receive from each student's success or lack thereof.

She wants to be a supporter rather than an evaluator. I feel more *open* to express my ideas and explore my own feelings. I can use my classroom in an experimental way and not worry constantly about evaluation.

She encourages creative teaching methods. This encourages me to *stretch* my thought processes and try new strategies. With the expectation for creativity, I don't feel that new experiences are too risky. I have been able to generate a whole series of learner activities for the fundamental skills course. She helps move the faculty beyond their comfort zone and the use of traditional teaching methods.

The principal's question, "What do you think you could have done better?" keeps me from becoming complacent with my planning from year to year. It keeps me *thinking*.

Because of her suggestions, I am much more inclined to *think* about and try new things without fear of failure.

The principal's acknowledgment of my creativity and risk taking encourage me to *persevere* and to *think, read,* and *converse* with others about new methods. Being a risk taker is not easy, and administrative support is crucial.

Praise. Praise focusing on specific and concrete teaching behaviors significantly fostered teacher reflection and reflectively informed behavior:

My principal's praise gets me *searching* for new and innovative things on my own. I am constantly *thinking* about innovative and creative things I can try with my classes regarding technology.

I conscientiously try to *utilize transition time* and wait time because she complimented me on it. I pay closer attention to wait time and transition time, which seems to increase my use even further.

She encourages me to find ways to use the strengths she saw in me to help the children learn. I use more *creative* strategies to teach that build on the children's strengths.

Praise motivates me to *think of new ideas.*

Other principal behaviors that enhanced teacher reflection and reflectively informed behavior included distributing professional literature, encouraging teachers to attend workshops and conferences, and encouraging collaboration with others (see Chapter 3 for a discussion of teacher reflection as a by-product of *staff development* programs and *collaboration* with others).

In sum, principal modeling, classroom observation, dialogue, suggestion, and praise have powerful effects on teacher reflection and reflectively informed behavior. Teachers explained that cognitive changes included being more open, self-analytical (critical), compassionate toward students, innovative, and creative. Specifically, changes in reflection included

- Increased *thinking* about instructional improvement, new ideas, innovative concepts
- A fresh *awareness* of student needs, instructional possibilities, potential of materials
- An enhanced problem-solving *orientation*
- An *openness* to new ideas and different approaches
- Attainment of new pedagogical *knowledge*
- A better *understanding* of self as practitioner
- A tendency to *self-analyze* and to consider one's strengths and weaknesses
- An improved *ability to learn* from one's mistakes
- Greater *willingness* to take risks
- Heightened *sensitivity* to others in the educational community

In addition, we found these major, reflectively informed *behavioral* changes in teaching:

- A tighter *focus* on student learning
- Increased instructional *variety* in the classroom

- Greater integration of concepts of *diversity* (e.g., multiple cultures) in instruction
- Better *planning and preparation* for teaching
- More *repetition* and enhancement of effective practices as revealed and reinforced in reflective conversations
- A greater sense of *discretion* over classroom decision making
- Increased *cooperation and collaboration* among teachers regarding instructional matters

Moreover, the principal behaviors of modeling, classroom observation, dialogue, suggestion, and praise had strong positive effects on teachers' motivation, self-esteem, confidence, and sense of security.

Cognitive Coaching: Bridge to Reflection

In Costa and Garmston's (1994) cognitive coaching model, instructional supervisors such as principals engage teachers in a supportive, *collegial* exploration of teaching and learning. Like many supervision models, cognitive coaching is growth oriented; however, it differs from most other models in that the evaluative steps are performed by the individual teacher. Figure 4.3 briefly outlines the cognitive coaching model. During collaborative, reflective discussions held by supervisors and teachers, teachers engage in the following types of activities:

- Recalling student behaviors from a class
- Comparing actual and desired student performance
- Making inferences
- Analyzing effects of teacher behaviors and making causal connections
- Evaluating appropriateness of teaching strategies
- Reflecting on one's thought processes
- Prescribing alternative strategies
- Employing metacognition (reflecting on, understanding, and controlling one's learning)

Cognitive Coaching

**A Structured Reflection Framework
for Building Professional Knowledge**

Cognitive Coaching enables teachers to deeply contemplate puzzling instructional problems with the help of a colleague.

1. Teaching is a complex, contextualized act of decision making.
2. Our perceptions guide our behavior.
3. Changing our behavior requires a change in perception (how we think).
4. Coaching can mediate changes toward more effective practice.

Goals of the Cognitive Coaching Model

1. Establishing and maintaining trust
2. Facilitating learning (including reflection on the lesson, using higher-order thinking skills, and self-analysis)
3. Enhancing growth toward cognitive autonomy (self-coaching and evaluation of one's performance)

*Elements of Professional Knowledge
in the Cognitive Coaching Model*

1. Building trust and rapport
2. Learning principles and knowledge construction (see, for example, extensive theoretical work by Bruner, Piaget, Taba, Knowles, Kohlberg, Fuller, Erikson, and Feuerstein)
3. Understanding how to use linguistic tools (e.g., questioning, wait time)
4. Expanding the coach's repertoire in building autonomous states of mind (teacher's efficacy, flexibility, clarity, consciousness, interdependence)

Figure 4.3. Cognitive Coaching

NOTE: For more on the cognitive coaching model, see A. L. Costa and R. J. Garmston (1994). (Videotapes and guidebooks about cognitive coaching are available from the Association for Supervision and Curriculum Development.)

Many of the teachers we studied reported that behaviors like those noted above occurred in their discussions with principals. In addition, they frequently linked what Costa and Garmston (1994) call maturing states of mind—that is, flexibility, efficacy, craftsmanship, interdependence, and consciousness—to principals' coaching. Costa and Garmston see these states of mind as catalysts that bring teachers to "increasingly authentic, congruent, ethical behavior, the touch-stones of integrity" (p. 131) and that eventually bring them to auton-omy *within* the organization, always a goal of supervising profession-als who are concerned with developing reflection in teachers:

> Autonomous individuals set personal goals and are self-directing, self-monitoring, and self-modifying. Because they are constantly experimenting and experiencing, they fail frequently, but they fail forward, learning from the situation. But autonomous persons are not isolated or mechanical in their work; rather, they also partici-pate significantly in their organization. They operate in the best interests of the whole while simultaneously attending to their own goals and needs. In other words they are at once independent and interdependent—they are holonomous. (p. 129)

Encouraging Reflection: Helpful Reminders

Reflection is a higher-order skill capable of producing large effects on classroom instruction and student learning. The good principals discussed in our research encouraged collaborative interactions by respecting the right of teachers to self-direction. Our findings about typical effective practices suggest the following reminders:

1. *Reflection is often a shared learning experience.* Reflection is, in essence, a complementary experience wherein both teacher and princi-pal acknowledge and use their collective expertise. Nolan (1989) notes that supervisors bring to this relationship

- Knowledge of observation techniques
- An ability to view the classroom from another teacher's per-spective
- Productive conferencing strategies
- Informed understanding of the teaching-learning process

Teachers bring

- Instructional skills
- Practical knowledge

- A willingness to examine beliefs and behavior
- An intimate knowledge of their particular environment

In essence, a vast collection of knowledge and skill can become available that nurtures teacher growth and benefits students if educators' interactions are not characterized by formal roles and senseless ground rules.

2. *Time must be allotted for reflective dialogue.* The normal hubbub of activity in schools leaves little time for thoughtful dialogue and professional reflection. Not surprisingly, educators are inclined to abandon efforts to reflect on practice when school life gets particularly hectic. They also find that it is difficult to switch to a thoughtful mode of discourse because they spend so much time isolated from other educators. Protected time for reflective dialogue is a prerequisite for teacher development; we found that often such time becomes available only through creative arrangements and determined effort.

3. *A lack of trust precludes reflection that might otherwise lead to school improvement.* Mutual observation and criticism require courage on the part of both principal and teacher because teaching is a complex, puzzling, and frequently unpredictable and surprising endeavor. The foundation for courage is grounded in trust between the principal and the teacher. A teacher's sense of being out of control, confused, and vulnerable (Schön, 1988) can often be mitigated by the feeling of being safe and respected by principals as the challenging work of reflecting on professional practice proceeds. Principals can establish cultural norms supporting collaboration, experimentation, risk taking, and continuous professional growth in a community of learners.

4. *Reflection is sense making.* In the reflective dialogue between principal and teacher, we learned that teachers essentially "research" their professional practice. They examine their thinking, make their professional knowledge explicit, and deeply explore complicated matters. Ultimately, they solve teaching problems by making sense of their thoughts and behaviors. A capable principal acknowledges the complexity and value of this struggle and strives to support the work of reflection by developing a capacity for collaborative dialogue.

5. *The ability to reflect must be developed over time.* The use of reflection to develop teaching expertise requires patience and perseverance.

It represents a slowly developed, complex blend of knowledge and skill derived from the following:

- Cognitive psychology (e.g., Frederiksen, 1984)
- Cognitive theory and information-processing theory (e.g., Sprint-hall, Reiman, & Thies-Sprinthall, 1996)
- Cognitive developmental theory (e.g., Berliner, 1988)
- Theories of reflection-in-action and guided reflection through dialogue (Schön, 1983; Vygotsky, 1930, 1933, 1935/1978)

In addition, some theorists argue that teachers should strive to reach the *highest* level of reflection, including recognition of critical political, social, and ethical issues that affect learning. These theorists readily acknowledge teachers' need for a solid base of *pedagogical* knowledge and skills in order to perform thoughtful critique of the work of schools, especially with regard to societal issues (e.g., gender, class, and ethnicity; see, e.g., Smyth, 1989). Calderhead (1987) found that student teachers, in particular, usually attain only the *lower* levels of reflection, which may be attributed to the following reasons:

- Inability to isolate specific teaching events upon which to reflect while engaged in practice
- Inability to be self-critical and acknowledge personal weaknesses when another's evaluation is crucial
- Inability to analyze one's own teaching critically, due to lack of experience and knowledge of alternative teaching practices

6. *The development of reflection skills requires verbal support and modeling.* Recent research (Glasner, 1997; Manning & Payne, 1996) reveals that verbal guidance and modeling of metacognitive and reflective thinking are critical to a teacher's development of reflection skills. This has implications not only for aspiring teachers, university supervisors, cooperating teachers, and teacher educators, but also for principals who supervise pedagogy and student academic achievement.

Clearly, reflection is a means of developing professional expertise (Short & Rinehart, 1993). The task of helping teachers learn to describe and understand their thinking, to think more critically and abstractly, rests in part with principals. An integration of knowledge and deep thought provokes better choices, better decision making, and an expanded knowledge base.

Portrait of a Facilitator for Reflective Practice

Osterman and Kottkamp (1993) aptly described the skills required for a position that might be found in today's schools. Indeed, these are the same skills we identified for the principals described in our study:

Position Available: Facilitator for Reflective Practice. A person who's inherently curious, someone who doesn't have all the answers and isn't afraid to admit it, someone who is confident enough in his or her ability to be able to accept challenges in a nondefensive manner; someone who is secure enough to make his or her own thinking public and therefore subject to discussion; someone who's a good listener; someone who likes and trusts other people to make the right decisions if given the opportunity; someone who is able to see things from another's perspective and is sensitive to the needs and feelings of others; someone who is able to relax and lean back and let others assume the responsibility for their own learning. Some experience desirable but not as important as the ability to learn from mistakes. (p. 64)

How Supervisors' Behaviors—
Positive and Negative—
Affect Teachers

5

Being Visible Versus Interrupting and Abandoning

In these three chapters comprising Part II of this book, we juxtapose our findings about the effects of positive, effective principal behaviors on classroom instruction with the effects of negative principal behaviors. These pages describe the good, the bad, and—at times—the ugly, with respect to leaders' actions and the impact of those actions on teachers.

This chapter discusses teachers' perspectives on three principal behaviors: *wandering around* (i.e., being visible) and, on the downside, *interruption* and *abandonment*. Insights into principals' purposes in enacting such behaviors and teachers' responses are also presented.

Visibility by Wandering Around

The good principals described in our study made informal visits to classrooms (often referred to as "walk-throughs"), and although these visits were usually unannounced, teachers viewed them very positively. During such visits principals typically observed teacher-student interaction and provided positive feedback. Teachers considered classroom visits as "customary" and "routine." In their view, the visits were nonthreatening and reflected principal interest in instruction as well as caring and respect for teachers:

My principal practices MBWA, *"management by wandering around."* She is an expert at informally observing both the classroom teachers and students, and she is very interested in what is happening within the school.

The principal *walks around* the school observing how teaching and learning are occurring. By this, we see concern for the students and for what we are doing. When there is something positive occurring, he tells us that we are doing well. I am honored that someone is interested in my well-being as a teacher and that someone helps keep me on course.

She is *in and out* of the classroom a great deal. The students and I are very comfortable with her presence. Since she is in the classroom so often, she knows what is going on and often provides supplementary information or materials or just helps me bounce around ideas.

My principal is a highly *visible* principal; he walks in and out of classrooms every day. I like it; it's a two-way street. He is there to see what's going on, but he is also putting himself out there to be called on for help or as a resource. Also, the students like knowing who their principal is, and I think there is a level of security created among staff and students by his consistent interaction in classrooms.

I am currently working for a new administrator who was placed at our school to "make changes." One way he does this is through visibility; he is *everywhere* all the time. In addition, he is an avid believer in making classroom visits. This is his way of checking with the teacher and observing what's going on.

During informal classroom visits, some principals interacted with teachers and students:

He stops by the classroom for a moment and spends some time *interacting* with my class. He will later provide positive feedback about my students, classroom, and my performance.

Although walk-throughs varied in length of time, most were rather brief, and many were followed up with a word or note of encouragement:

He *stops in* the room for short periods of time—just to watch—for maybe five minutes. Later in the day he acknowledges something he saw or writes me a *quick note*. These have been nonthreatening for me.

He would *drop by* frequently for informal visits to my classroom. These would be short, three to five minutes. Any observations he had from this time would be shared with me at a later time. There is no threat because there are no written evaluations. Most comments were positive: "I like to see the hands-on activity" or "the students are working well together in groups!" At first this was scary because I had never had another principal do this. Then I realized he wasn't interested in trying to catch me doing something wrong.

After an observation—mainly the informal ones—she *drops a note* in my mailbox about positive things she saw in the classroom or connects on improvements she sees that students are making.

He gives positive feedback in the form of *notes after walk-throughs*. These include detailed information on effective teaching practices.

She visits my classroom while I am teaching and observes me. Before she leaves, if she likes what I've done, she *comments* to me or praises me and the students.

During walk-throughs, principals even offered teachers constructive criticism, although this happened very infrequently:

The principal visits the classroom unannounced and sits in on a lesson. He makes no verbal comments but leaves a note of *constructive criticism* on methods that he thinks work also. He always ends with a positive comment. I know he cares about the students I teach and is interested in their success.

Good principals also visited teachers after school hours to discuss instruction:

Mr. Swanson frequently stops by my room to converse. When I'm there late and he's there late, he'll *swing by* before leaving. One night he stopped by while I was grading student projects using a recently developed rubric. We began discussing a low-functioning student and his success on this assignment, a map creation. Mr. _____ looked at all the projects and the rubric and praised the kids' efforts. The next morning he stopped by the room to tell all the kids he's proud of their efforts. They beam, and I'm pleased. Success breeds success.

Principals attended special events and provided positive feedback to teachers:

He will *attend* some activities that we have going on, and the next day he is always very positive about what he saw. He will *tell* my students how proud he is of us. After attending a cattle show, he said that the cattle we were showing were much better quality than when he taught agriculture.

My principal takes note and acknowledges the positive things I do. For example, he is always *in attendance* when my students and I play for the district concert festival. Participating in this event is optional. However, it has had a positive influence on my students' musical growth. His support influences my decision to continue to participate.

My principal was a music teacher prior to her present assignment. I was fearful that she would be critical of my work. However, she uses her experience to encourage and support me. She *visits* my class often and praises the students. She is *at every concert*. She often asks how she can facilitate my programs. She is encouraging, supportive, and facilitative.

Why Is He or She Wandering Around?

Teachers in our study speculated that principals used informal class visits to achieve several distinct purposes:

- *To motivate teachers*

Her goal is to get me charged up and to get my students charged up.

. . . to get me to do more and to provide more opportunities for the students.

- *To monitor instruction*

. . . to see that students get the best possible instruction in a safe, healthy environment, because attempting to save all of the children is the number-one priority of a principal.

. . . to see that teachers teach their best every day.

- *To be accessible and provide support*

He knows life is not always positive for the risk taker; because some colleagues are not supportive, administrative support is crucial.

I think she wants to be involved as much as possible, to provide as much help and support as possible.

- *To keep informed*

She wants to keep her thumb on the pulse of activities in the school.

She wants knowledge about what's actually going on, and she wants input into it.

Less frequently, teachers reported that principals visited classrooms with the specific purpose of enhancing teacher morale; interestingly, increases in teacher morale did result from informal visits.

The Impact of Wandering Around

According to our data, wandering around enhanced teachers' *motivation, self-esteem, sense of security,* and, as already mentioned, *morale.* In particular, wandering around was strongly linked to the reinforcement of existing good teaching behavior; reflection and reflectively informed behavior were usually *not* noticeably affected:

Every time she takes time to stop in my room, I feel that my teaching really does matter to her. It tells me that what I'm doing is important. . . . This keeps me *focused on* my teaching at all times. Her surprise drop-ins are a chance for her to see that there are many things going on at all times, not just during formal observations.

When a person praises me for a job well done, it makes me *work harder.* . . . I have put on two shows this year where we have given away more than $1,000 in prize money. It never helps to put someone down. . . . Say something nice or do not say anything.

Her feedback makes me think that I'm appreciated. I feel *lifted in spirit* and keep working hard.

These visits help me to keep a *focus* and to always *be ready.* I always think about teaching in a structured way in which I feel the students are learning and progressing but also in a way that an administrator would feel good observing.

I think about how I can use the technique she likes in other areas or ways. For example, I'm using measurement manipulatives and trying to relate problems and activities to the real world. I want to be a better teacher so I do what I believe is good to do, but when the principal agrees with what I'm doing it *reinforces* my thoughts and so I continue to do certain things.

I started inviting him in for visits. Of course, I began *doing more of the things* that he made positive comments about. I also *focused* on those students that he saw having behavioral problems. I didn't find him a threat, but he could have been more effective by letting teachers know he was going to be in their wing.

I know I had better be on my toes, and at the same time I'm glad he is in and out of the classroom because if I need help, he's there to help me to *stay on task* better, and I have a more positive attitude toward teaching. You don't want to make a bad impression on your boss, and you want him to see you teaching and appreciate what you're doing.

When wandering around affected teacher reflection and reflectively informed behavior, the impacts were significant:

Because of her supportive visits, I am much *more relaxed* about the music I choose and the management of my classroom. I feel free to *develop my own curriculum* and tailor it to the needs and desires of each group of students. Students no longer push buttons, and I have learned not to take their behaviors and comments personally. It has made me a *calmer, more relaxed,* and more productive teacher. Because of her positive attitude, our entire staff is this way. She helps us to do all the small things better and to see the big picture.

His visits tell me he cares about the students I teach and is interested in their success. This makes me want *to do a better job* and encourages me *to get input* from others and have an open mind. His personal interest makes me feel what I do is important.

She is in and out of the classroom a great deal. This strategy makes me more *confident* in my teaching because she *reinforces* or constructively criticizes in a way that makes me want to excel. She makes me *examine* my own strategies and think about all aspects of my teaching. It makes me *plan* more thoroughly; I do the necessary research and gather needed materials.

Interruption of Class Instruction

We also found that walking around had a downside: Ineffective principals actually interrupted and interfered with teachers in their classrooms. Some visited classes unannounced and attempted to correct problems they observed:

My principal drops into class and tells us how to do things. He *interrupts* and tries to add to our teaching while you are teaching.

He enters the room after I've started my lessons and *tries to correct* a situation on the spot. He'll *pull me aside* and mention a better way to instruct that lesson. I find it nerve-wracking.

On one occasion the principal actually *took over* the class. I had been demonstrating a particular task, and it seemed to me and my students that she wanted to show that she could perform the task better.

In addition, ineffective principals, according to our data, also visited classes during instruction to make announcements or "chat" with students:

He comes in while I am teaching to *personally hand me the announcement* sheet and will talk about various things that aren't essential at that moment.

He *walks into class* at anytime and just *starts talking* to the kids. . . . He never acknowledges the teacher.

At other times, such principals required teachers to meet with them during instructional time or scheduled events and required classes to attend:

She tends to like to talk a lot. Often she *calls me into her office* and talks for an hour before she tells me why I'm there. She should come talk to me on my lunch break rather than call me away from my kids.

My principal has a difficult time making decisions. Scheduling, discipline, and curriculum changes are either ignored or not taken seriously. The last two Fridays he has changed the schedules to put on an *"impromptu" spirit assembly*. Even though a majority of faculty members complained the first time he did this, the next week the same thing happened.

Ineffective principals also interrupted classes with intercom announcements and sometimes did so in very negative ways:

The principal *constantly interrupts* on the loudspeaker at unscheduled times and notifies us of special programs at the last minute so our lesson plans are ineffectual.

The principal has a terrible habit of communicating his thoughts to teachers by *using the speaker* during class. He will "get on" [criticize] teachers in front of the students by using the speaker.

Reasons for Interruption

Teachers felt that principals interrupted classes to *demonstrate power* ("It's a power move of authority. It puts everyone on alert that she is present"), to *monitor* ("I believe that she wants to know that students and teachers are on task"), and to *inform* ("to let me know the news of the day"). Several teachers stated that their principals probably had "no goals" in interrupting classes and explained that they simply had *no impulse control.*

The Impact of Interruptions

Overwhelmingly, teachers disclosed that being interrupted during instructional time provoked deep anger:

The frequent interruptions have always been a terrible, unnecessary waste of precious teaching and learning time. I tend to disregard announcements made on the intercom. I make sure to wait till the last possible moment to go to assemblies, trying to seat my class near the back door to make a speedy getaway. It isn't effective, it *drives me nuts,* and it makes me feel *angry and resentful* and *irritated.* It makes me *feel crazy, aggravated,* and *frustrated.*

It is *frustrating,* and it makes me *angry.* It is difficult for me to concentrate on class. I usually am quite flexible, but this constant disruption is quite difficult to deal with.

Class interruptions *lessen my authority* with students and lower teacher morale. It is a *terrible* method.

Upon hearing that 55 of her 65 teachers had requested a transfer she said, "Well, that's their problem—they just can't understand me." Talk about a *lot of anger and resentment.* I'm on the verge of resigning—I've requested a transfer. If this is the kind of leader our universities are producing, no wonder education is failing miserably.

My principal comes in and out of class and speaks. I am *not* pleased to have my teaching routine upset, especially when he simply stands at the door watching. I feel *spied* upon and *mistrusted.*

He comes in while I am teaching; it *disrupts* me and *distracts* my students. It breaks their attention, and I have to take time to get it back. It wastes time without reason. *I can't stand it.*

Sometimes he would correct a situation on the spot. He'd pull me aside and mention a better way to instruct that lesson. I *become nervous.* I lose my place or train of thought. I speak under my breath, Why now? Why me? I recoup and try harder to please the principal. I begin "acting"—teaching for him and not the students.

She interrupts and adds to your teaching while you are teaching. I *feel nervous*, like she has no trust in what I'm doing. It breaks my concentration. *I dislike it*!

Abandonment

Also on the downside, we found that many of the ineffective principals described by teachers in our study made no (or few) informal visits to classrooms. In other words, being visible—whether wandering around or interrupting—had more positive than negative effects, but *not* being visible was more likely to be construed negatively (what we refer to as *abandonment*) rather than positively (as in the case of autonomy; see Chapter 7).

Making no (or few informal) classroom visits is not, of course, a behavior principals use to influence teachers; instead it reveals a principal's total unwillingness to assume responsibility for instructional leadership:

The principal is *not involved* in the school, and he *does not even visit* my classroom.

She *doesn't come into* the classroom enough. It makes you feel she doesn't care or have time for you. It must take away from her priorities. She comes to you only when asked, and it makes you feel that you are at the bottom of her list.

Most of the days the principal is *not even in the building* to help teachers. She says she's at principals' meetings.

The principal *never visited* my classroom. We never discussed my teaching. When I tried to approach him to discuss my teaching, he would always just nod and say "good"; he showed no real interest.

The principal *never comes* into my room except for the yearly evaluation. It's a waste of time, mine and his.

My principal *isn't involved* in instruction. By not getting involved, he's sending a message to his teachers that what goes on in the classroom is unimportant to him.

She is *not visible* throughout the school and never observes classes unless performing a formal observation, but I see her wasting time on non-job-related activities.

Honestly, I had a hard time coming up with a positive strategy used by my principal. He does not do or say anything that affects me positively. In the two years I have been at my school, he *has visited my classroom once.* He does *not stop* by the classroom to talk or visit; he *does not engage* me in conversations concerning instructional matters; and I can think of nothing in the realm of policies that he has put in place which affects my teaching. Sorry, my principal doesn't really supervise me instructionally.

My principal *never comes* into my room to see what we are doing. I like the fact that he doesn't bug me because he's such a power-hungry ego-tripper.

Reasons for No (or Few) Visits

Most teachers who discussed principals' failure to make informal classroom visits could associate *no goals* with this approach. Several reported that their principals were dominated by *noninstructional concerns*: "She is too busy to care about instruction." In some instances, *avoidance of work* was discussed as a goal: "The less she involves herself, the less she has to do or worry about." Two teachers explained that their principals chose not to visit their classrooms to prevent *interference*: "She doesn't want to interfere or make you feel nervous." But, these same teachers interpreted their principals' behavior as reflecting a "lack of caring." (Teachers did *not* associate their principal's lack of class visits with encouraging autonomy.)

In addition to not making classroom visits, some principals, teachers reported, were *completely ineffective* as instructional leaders. They did nothing at all with regard to, for example, staff development, instructionally focused meetings, curriculum development, or action research to support classroom instruction:

> My principal doesn't do anything at all to help me with instruction. He *rarely comes in* the classroom to see my kids, and he doesn't offer any assistance with my instruction.

> My principal has *very little* to do with what I am doing in the classroom. He uses a very *laissez-faire approach* to leadership. I would welcome any new strategies or techniques. Teachers who have been out of the university setting for a long time especially need these. By not getting involved in instruction, he is sending a message that what goes on in the classroom is unimportant to him.

> My principal is a hard person to make contact with. If you do, she *never gets back* to you.

> My school is in chaos. The principal will retire this year. He wants no conflict, and he has *no interest* at all in instruction.

> Our principal seems to be more involved in the business of running the school and *not concerned* with individual teaching styles.

> My principal mainly deals with discipline referrals. She has *little time* to actually help with instruction.

> My principal *doesn't address* instructional issues directly. He has no specific goals related to instruction.

In the last 6 years I have worked in two different elementary schools. Both principals *left me completely* alone to teach as I wanted; *neither did anything to* influence my teaching. I was a very strong teacher with positive and definite ideas about what was good teaching, but it's a sad commentary that my instructional leaders have *done nothing* to influence me.

This person sat in the library, ate doughnuts, and read the newspaper. I *rarely saw* him. We had major problems at our school that he chose to ignore. He was just putting in his time.

The teachers who discussed this do-nothing approach to instruction stated that their principal had *no goals*. Several teachers made cynical comments such as "She is retiring at the end of the year; that is her goal" and "He is too concerned about his own image to be concerned about the education that is going on in the classroom."

Impact on Teachers

Overwhelmingly, teachers who reported that their principal does nothing as an instructional leader described major adverse effects on *motivation* and *self-esteem*, as well as significant increases in *anger*, *psychic pain*, and feelings of being *unsupported*. Some tried to assuage their sense of abandonment with support from other sources, but many simply tried to *avoid* their principal altogether:

Professionally, I don't even consider my principal. I just *never* have the opportunity to ask his opinion on instructional issues. He gets paid an awful lot for doing nothing; the phrase "feeding at the public trough" comes to mind.

I would welcome any suggestions for new strategies or techniques. We basically *set our own* goals; sometimes they're not related to instruction. Most teachers *need* guidance and instructional leadership. My principal is very weak in this capacity.

I asked her last October to help me get started with my intern, and she has yet to get back to me. I *won't go to her* for anything else. There are no results. She is lazy and doesn't care about helping her teachers.

I have *minimal contact* with my principal. This has been confusing. It has caused me to be relaxed, not concerned about details. I have to *develop myself* because there are no external stimuli to do so. I need more support.

I get *no support,* no analysis, no interaction, no development. I'm totally *independent.* My professional development comes from other sources.

I feel very *isolated* in my job. There's no accountability. I tend to be *too relaxed*—occasionally *not prepared* for class.

Since my principal isn't involved in instruction, *I always wonder* if I'm doing an OK job with my teaching. He never observes me so I have no idea. I really wish my principal would become more involved with me and my students.

I *never felt valued* by him as a teacher. He is too concerned about his own image to be concerned about the education that is going on in the classroom. I *hate it.*

I guess her strategy is "If it ain't broke, don't fix it." My principal is just a figurehead for my evaluations. Maybe my department head should serve as my instructional supervisor. It would help.

In addition, lack of instructional leadership frequently resulted in a *loss of teachers' respect* for the principal and *subpar performance* by teachers, especially among those who had become jaded:

It makes me *angry.* I think that she is less professional than she should be. She doesn't *really* care about what goes on in classrooms as long as it "looks good" or presents no problems for her. Ignore her. I chose to be a great teacher and swear to myself that I will know what goes on in my building when I become a principal. I look to her as a leader, and she is just not there. I lead myself.

I feel like she is not very interested in me, in how or why I'm teaching what I'm teaching. I may *become lax* on certain days and allow more free time than I should.

It seems that he is uninterested in what we do in the classroom. I have, at times, *become lax* about things I am normally on top of. It truly *saddens* and *frustrates* me.

I like to have feedback several times during the year; I might be a *better* teacher if she were present more often. She makes me *angry*—she is lazy.

It makes me think that he doesn't care about my program and the hard work I do. So, I *don't try as hard* or search for new teaching methods.

We are *not an important part* of the school so we do not warrant his time or consideration. At times we almost seem to *give up*; what does it matter that we handle almost all of our discipline problems? We know that the principal does not care what we are doing. We feel *left out*, out on a limb most of the time. What happens when we really need guidance?

I'm pretty much convinced that my principal did not influence my teaching; most of what influenced me I gleaned from professional journals, other effective teachers, and reflecting on methods and strategies. It's a *sad commentary* that my instructional leader has done very little to influence me.

Clearly, the educational influence of the visible principal, the principal who grants professional autonomy to teachers but who also walks around the school supporting their instructional efforts, far surpasses that of the principal who abandons teachers. Working with teachers as an interested, caring, supportive educator is the hallmark of instructional leadership, and the rewards of such efforts accrue to students, teachers, and principals alike.

Praising Versus Criticizing

What importance do teachers attribute to a principal's praise and a principal's criticism? Teachers' intense responses to these divergent behaviors directly influence classroom instruction. This chapter begins with a discussion of our findings about praise.

Praise

We found that goods principals typically praised teachers in *formal* interactions, for example, during postobservation conferences. In *informal* interactions, praise, which was more often than not given orally, was usually *general* rather than *specific*. It was less detailed than it was when given during informal class walk-throughs and formal postobservation conferences. In both cases, praise represents a principal's overall positive *reaction* to a teacher's or a group of teachers' instructional performance. Praise was *not* always coupled with concrete feedback or suggestions for instructional improvement. One teacher's story demonstrates the dramatic effect that praise held for many of the teachers we studied:

During the 6 years I have worked with my principal, I have always felt that she saw great potential in me. My successes thrilled her, and she praised me both publicly and privately. She even became a mentor to me. We weren't buddies who went out for a drink after work, but she became someone who believed in me and encouraged me. There were no hidden agendas in our relationship, only our mutual desire for me to be the very best I could be for myself and for the children in the school. If I could pinpoint one powerful effect of her behavior, it would be the way her praise felt like a gift. She would call me in and tell me that she heard good things about my class or my teaching, and she thought how much I might enjoy hearing this. She would make me feel it was a great opportunity for me to be a teacher.

Praise With Positive Effects

Praise Given Privately

Several types of praise (e.g., congratulations and commendations, words of reinforcement, and outright compliments) were given by principals in informal interactions with teachers (i.e., in private conversations or notes). Such approaches to praise send a valuable and powerful message to teachers:

> The principal constantly *reminds me* of the difference I've made in the lives of students. When I go into her office with a referral or problem with a student, she encourages me and reminds me how much faith she has in my ability to handle students with behavior needs.

> She gives me positive *comments* like, "You are a good teacher," or *writes* complimentary notes on things that I've done well. When she is pleased with something I am doing, she *tells* me what she believes is good and effective.

> Just last night I had a parent night, and she *came in* for a few minutes. This morning I had a positive, detailed *note* praising me for my efforts.

> My principal stops me in the hall and *tells* me something good that she thinks I'm doing. Sometimes she notices something good my students have done and relates it to me. That feels good. It is always private praise or encouragement, and I like it that way.

He *stops me* when I'm on-the-go and informally says, "Hey, good job on that!" These frequent pats on the back really help on a daily basis.

Principals often praised teachers when they took risks with innovative instruction:

She praised my attempts to *try new ideas* in the classroom. When they were not effective, she didn't make me feel like I had failed.

Sometimes principals praised individual teachers by relaying positive comments made by parents:

She will often tell me what a *parent* has told her about me.

My principal passes on comments made by *parents* as to the effectiveness of my instruction. He would quote them. Everyone likes to believe someone is noticing their efforts. Parents can be extremely critical and are often ignorant about what is actually going on in the classroom. The fact that parents feel positive about instruction indicates that their children are giving them a positive view of classroom activities.

Praise Given Publicly

Frequently, principals praised individual teachers publicly and informally, usually at faculty meetings or on the school intercom:

She *speaks* well of me, pointing out my good work in front of other teachers.

My principal praised me for working very hard with a special-needs child who had significant behavior challenges in my regular classroom and not giving up on that child. He did this in front of the entire faculty at a *faculty meeting*.

My principal praises me *directly* in a group setting. He also thanks me for doing things or going that extra mile. He is very appreciative of us and what we do.

He recognizes faculty members *publicly* and personally when members of the faculty have accomplished some of their goal or have gone beyond the norm in performing routine tasks.

My principal will often *announce* the positive contributions that teachers have made within their classroom or throughout the school over the P.A. system.

At times, principals praised individual teachers in front of students and parents:

My principal is constantly bragging about me to the *community*. Once she told a parent that I was one of the best teachers. This comment was made in my presence.

She talks with *parents and students* about my attributes, skills, and abilities.

He uses praise informally, both directly to me and also indirectly. When he praises indirectly, it is usually by coming into my classroom and talking to the *students* about how great the class is!

Principals praised groups of teachers in public settings as well:

She always opens every *meeting* with positive remarks. It is almost like faculty meetings are a pep rally! She really highlights the positive. She says things like, "You are the best faculty ever," or "When I compare notes with other principals, I know I am so lucky to have a staff as motivated and talented as you are."

He always gives a specific positive comment about each of four or five teachers at *faculty meetings*.

He likes to *refer* to the Special Education Department as being one of the best in the region. In our accreditation meeting last week, our department was commended for outstanding services. He praised us for our work. His appreciation does influence our teaching, and we try very hard to keep our fine reputation alive.

Why Is He or She Praising Teachers?

Teachers in our study disclosed that good principals praised them for several reasons:

- *To motivate and to reward*

I think he wants to show that hard work and persistence do pay off.

His goal is to have each teacher reach his/her potential and peak of effectiveness.

Positive yields positive. Teachers who feel good about their work perform better and yield better instructional results.

- *To enhance self-esteem*

He's trying to boost morale and individual self-esteem.

- *To demonstrate caring*

The goal is for the teacher to know that the principal does care about the teacher and about what goes on in the classroom.

- *To gain compliance with expectations*

He wanted me to know what he thought was important: to continue using wait time and making good transitions during lessons.

As a footnote, we found one teacher who viewed a principal's purpose in praising her as patronizing; however, she still appreciated it:

I think he thinks I need to be thanked like a child, but I still value his doing it, regardless of his goals.

The Impact of Praise

Most frequently, principals' praise positively and strongly affected teachers' *motivation, self-esteem,* and *confidence.* We also learned that although praise had a strong effect on teachers by *reinforcing* existing positive classroom behaviors, it had lesser effects on their reflection and reflectively informed behavior. Teachers reported:

> His praise made me *want to continue* to work hard with all of my students because hard work does not go unnoticed. Praise made me *feel that teaching was worth every struggle* and that you must endure and not give up so easily. It also made me realize that all students don't have to be doing the same thing to learn. Sometimes as teachers we get into a rut, feeling like that.

> Praise made me *feel* as if I was doing a good job and that I was *appreciated*.

> Praise *motivated me* to continue positive behavior and to *work even harder*. Praise lets you know you're appreciated.

> Praise made me *feel good*, feel that I was noticed and important, that I had done something positive. It made me want to continue to *try harder* to do a better job.

> Shortly after receiving praise, I feel *energized*. I'm so peppy that the students see me jumping around the room full of energy. Praise is an excellent means of motivation.

> As a teacher, I want my administrator to know and to recognize that I am trying to perform my duties in a way that enhances student achievement. When I am *affirmed* by the administrator, it assures me that I am acting appropriately. It creates a *desire* in me to *continue* to perform at an even higher level.

> My current principal's remarks give me validation that I am a good teacher. He builds my *self-esteem* and gives me *confidence*. He makes me feel *valued* and needed. My previous principal had, in three years of poor leadership and negative responses, almost totally destroyed my self-esteem and value as a teacher. My current principal has restored my faith in myself and has allowed me to teach my way.

I have more *confidence* in my ability because I know she thinks I'm doing a great job. I certainly wouldn't want to disappoint her or give her any reason to question her opinion of me.

Her strategy made me more *positive* in the classroom. I spend more time praising and finding the children's strengths. I praise more often. I bring *more love and caring* to the classroom. She makes me feel very important and valued. I come to work to do my best. I want to live up to her high regard.

Once my principal announced his appreciation of my efforts to help facilitate the dismissal of students outside the campus over the P.A. system. This prompted me to continue my efforts. He made me feel *appreciated*. I was confident that he was behind my approach/concern for the children. Teachers *love to hear their names* called over the speaker in appreciation.

I began to *plan lessons in the hopes* of being recognized again.

Praise With Negative Effects

Unauthentic and Inappropriate Praise

Some ineffective principals used *unauthentic* (i.e., insincere) and/or *inappropriate* forms of praise with teachers. Unauthentic praise was perceived as perilously close, in terms of negative effects, to outright criticism (see next section for more about criticism): "Sometimes I feel he says one thing to my face and another behind my back." "I didn't feel he was always sincere in everything he said." "This strategy is OK, but I just feel he tries to say something positive; it's hard to know how he really feels." "I wonder how often negative comments are not shared." Praise was also defined as unauthentic when it was given in a perfunctory manner and when it was neither informed by knowledge of nor linked specifically to teachers' instruction:

For praise to be an effective motivator, it should specifically address a classroom technique or strategy, and it should not be given as a generic pat on the back. I would like my principal to be aware of my teaching. I don't know for sure that he is even aware of the content of my course. *This isn't true praise.*

Praise was also considered unauthentic when it was viewed as manipulative:

> Our principal used to drive me crazy over her concern about how we looked to others. She was very proud of the work my team of seventh grade teachers was doing; consequently, she showed us off to every visitor, the [local] school board members, the county commissioners, and the state school board members; even the lieutenant governor came by! *We felt like dancing dogs* after awhile: Wind us up and let us teach. While it was great to be recognized for what we were doing, we began to wonder if it was for the right reasons. We wanted to try other strategies and focus more on different aspects of students' needs but felt we needed to stay on task and continue to perform as expected so as not to let the principal down. In reality we did not grow professionally, and we feel our students did not get our best.

Some teachers defined praise as *inappropriate* (although it might have been authentic) when it was given to certain teachers but not others at faculty meetings, particularly when the teachers singled out were felt to be undeserving of such praise:

> He praises the *multimedia* program in front of the whole faculty. He means well, but actually this really irritates other teachers to the point that they are openly hostile.

Many teachers who discussed ineffective principals' unauthentic and inappropriate praise stated it was used to *motivate* them to work harder but "in a controlling way." Teachers also believed that many ineffective principals were probably unaware of the negative impacts of this behavior. Many teachers in the study sample who discussed negative forms of praise reported that their principal often used this technique to pursue *self-serving* goals ("to be recognized as a model school administrator"). The remaining teachers in our study offered no description of principals' goals with regard to the use of unauthentic and inappropriate praise.

Negative forms of principal praise adversely affected teacher self-esteem and increased teacher anger, frustration, and a sense of futility; teachers also lost trust in their principals. Other negative effects included teacher avoidance of and resistance to principals and reduced communication with the principal.

Favoritism: One Person's Reward

Teachers reported that some ineffective principals used two forms of *favoritism* as a strategy to control them. First, principals *consulted only with select individuals or groups* in making decisions:

> My principal will go to the *same group* of people to gather ideas. She will discuss her ideas with that group and then tell the other groups what to do.

> She has her *favorites,* and they make the decisions. I don't go to her for anything; I just don't care too much anymore.

> My principal sometimes makes decisions concerning programs directly involving teachers without consulting the faculty from the grades using the programs. Often decisions are made because of one or two *favored* teachers. It is ridiculous to scrap an entire program to pacify one teacher who may be incompetent, lazy, or tired of the program. I feel resentment. The grapevine kicks in, and I dig in my heels and resist the decision.

Second, principals were labeled as "playing favorites" when they *rewarded* and praised teachers *unfairly:*

> At my school the principal *recognizes the lazy* teachers for the simplest things they do. This is offensive. I work very hard. I feel like I'm being taken for granted.

> My principal attempts to publicly praise persons for a job well done, but she focuses on the *same* people time and again and neglects the other 90% of the faculty, leading them to doubt their own effectiveness. I really question any praise she gives me, and I analyze it to see what's in it for her. I continue to do my job, but I never expect anything from her. I have no trust in her anymore.

Criticism: More About Control

The flip side of principal praise is criticism. We found that principal criticism directly and indirectly affects teachers' classroom performance. For example, criticism had substantial negative effects on teacher morale and indirect, but strong, negative effects on teachers' instructional behavior.

Private Criticism of Individual Teachers

Several ways of giving private criticism were apparent in our data. Ineffective principals placed *notes* in teachers' mailboxes accusing them of wrongdoing in their classrooms:

> He puts *notes* in teachers' boxes every morning when he thinks you have done something wrong or something he doesn't like. I check my box religiously.

> My principal is a very autocratic leader and one of complete "power over" philosophy. She places little *"nasty-grams"* in your box. For example: "You were observed allowing a student to enter your room after the bell." This is followed by an explanation of all the reasons why you should not do that.

> He likes to hand out *"see me"* notes.

Principals communicated criticism toward individual teachers through negative *affect*:

> My principal is very short-tempered and mean-spirited. She likes to control and belittle. Sometimes she gets carried away and *raises her voice* at you at the wrong time and place.

> She sits at her desk when I come into her office and looks up *without saying anything.* She waits for me to speak, not asking me to sit down or saying anything to me. It's awful . . . has she got a problem! The bitch!

She looks at you with no expression, asks a string of probing questions without explanations, and *leaves you hanging.*

Her *attitude* toward others is demeaning and inappropriate for the workplace.

My principal gives *negative looks* while walking by my classroom that make you feel completely inadequate. Many teachers think these looks are intentional.

His requests are made in an offensive, demanding *tone* and with ultimatums.

To compound matters, our data point out that ineffective principals who criticized teachers privately often *failed to provide them with alternative suggestions to what they were doing* ("He does not guide but strictly comes down on those who do not know what to do") *and threatened* them instead:

My principal called me to her office to tell me how "disappointed" she was in me for asking, in front of others, for the air conditioning to be turned on. She *shook her finger* in my face and told me to "be careful."

After the principal criticizes you because he doesn't like certain actions or behaviors, the *threat of documentation* is also made.

He tends to criticize for minor mistakes and then uses *threats* to impose his power.

Some principals even criticized teachers before investigating problems:

In that I rarely see my principal, I find it difficult when I am called to see him to discover that it is always about something he assumes is *negative*. He has been known to rebuke me or others on the word of a student, never bothering to *get my side.*

He reacts with hostility *without* first getting *the facts.*

One ineffective principal described in our study cited a third party—in this case, a parent—to support his criticism of a teacher:

> After I had disagreed with him on a policy, he called me into his office and said he had received a call from a parent saying I had raised my voice with the children. I told him I had a hard time imagining this and asked him to set up a conference with the parent so we could clear the air. My principal said that he couldn't set up a conference because he had promised them confidentiality. I never heard any more about this. I never believed him. The next year he changed the policy I disagreed with; he just *had to be in control*. He didn't like teachers to point out that something should be done differently.

Other tactics principals employed to convey their criticism included "playing devil's advocate," "being extremely inquisitive," saying "when I taught, I did it this way," and "being overly critical—not constructive—about [the teacher's] behavior."

Principals' Goals Related to Private Criticism

In the teachers' view, one of the goals of principals who engaged in negative and even hostile private criticism was to *demonstrate power*; that is, power was seen as an end in itself:

> I really felt that the reason he was so critical was to find something wrong. When he found something wrong, he felt *powerful*.

> He uses criticism to instill fear, to show who's *boss*!

> He is critical because he truly enjoys the *power* he holds over others.

Teachers also indicated that *control* (i.e., teacher *compliance*) was a major goal of many principals who privately criticized them:

> The principal wants *everyone in line* and everyone to play by the rules.

> He does this to keep *everyone on top of things*.

He was trying to *put me in my place,* but I'm still outspoken on certain issues. I try to be more diplomatic when I approach him about change.

In a few instances, the goal of using criticism was to increase teacher *motivation* and *efficiency*: "He tries to resolve problems quickly." Several teachers reported that they viewed private criticism as "irrational" and *without goals*: "There is *no* goal attached to her personal hostility." "There is not a goal. It's a reaction."

The Effects of Private Criticism

We found that private criticism by principals had devastating effects on teachers and their performance. Teachers reported major negative impacts on *motivation, self-esteem,* and *morale*; increases in *fearfulness* and *confusion*; and strong adverse effects on *respect* for the principal and, to a lesser degree, on *trust* for the principal. Major *behavioral* impacts included increases in teacher *compliance, ignoring, avoidance, resistance/rebellion,* and *cautiousness*. Increases in *interference* with teaching, reflection, and reflectively informed behavior were other primary effects of private criticism. The following comments illustrate several of the negative effects noted above:

Teachers become very *uncooperative;* they don't do well if they are being "called on the carpet."

I feel like I *can't trust* her because of her insecurities. I would rather have a supervisor who respects me and is my teacher. A supervisor should guide teachers to come up with strategies for self-development, not just dictate and criticize.

These autocratic behaviors have a negative effect on the climate of the school. Low teacher *morale* and low student morale are present. The teachers prefer not to have any contact [with the principal]. This has had a negative effect in that no new strategies are going to take place.

This method of interacting has a negative impact on my thoughts and behavior. I am *less motivated, less productive.*

What I think *can't be printed*! I shut down and cease to participate in extra activities at school. The overall climate of the school was ruined.

I *feel rather small* at times. I avoid him in general. I asked for a transfer.

I *lose respect* for the principal when he criticizes me and my children.

This type of negative, noninformative method is not effective with my personality. It puts me *on the defensive.*

His accusing manner belittles me, destroys my confidence, and takes away my enjoyment of teaching. I *hate* and *resent* it!

We never have a good discussion about an issue or a decision. I try to stay away from him as much as possible. I am always *on guard.* It upsets me.

It *narrows* my actions to the level of making sure the details the principal is watching are covered.

It reduces risk taking and professional exploration. I take the *safe road.* It is a poor way to direct the human resources and energy of a system to foster growth. It creates *anger* and *resentment* toward the supervisor and the process.

He puts me on the *defensive;* when put on the defensive, no one wants to change. It *angers* me and the rest of the staff.

I think, "What is she after?" What is her problem? *Bitch!* How soon can I leave this school? Volunteer nothing. Ask no questions. She is not getting out of me what she wants if she wants more than just enjoying her power.

Later I think, "You *bitch!* That's awful. Pardon me for living." I really wish I didn't have to see her, believe me. She interfered with my performance. I had to think too much about her when I should have been thinking about my students. I have defensive feelings, *cold* feelings. I feel *sad*. It's a shame we can't work together.

This strategy makes me dislike my supervisor. I begin to think more about what I'm doing wrong than what I should do for students. I am very careful to keep from doing anything wrong. I take no chances and play it safe. It makes me *apathetic*. It makes me *want to leave*.

It causes me to be more *rebellious* and take more time in completing the tasks given me.

I keep on going despite his criticisms, moodiness, and lack of caring. Fortunately, I'm one of those people who doesn't need a lot of reinforcement. For a lot of faculty members and secretarial staff, his demeanor is very *detrimental*. It's sad; I don't think he realizes how moody he is. The office secretaries have told us he never compliments or thanks them. He never makes any attempts to recognize his staff on holidays. The secretaries will often remark on a particular day, "Watch out, he's on the rag again"— which means everyone is fair game for one of his nasty verbal remarks. One day I observed him carrying the book *The Seven Habits of Highly Effective People*!

She rarely tells you that you are doing a good job, but she certainly lets you know if she thinks you aren't performing well. For her to consider me a successful teacher, she thinks I should have dead silence in my room. I became so *stressed out* when my students spoke that I loaded them down with work so they wouldn't talk. I understand that order has a place in the classroom; however, there are times when experimentation and discovery are also appropriate. She doesn't tolerate differing views on classroom management.

Public Criticism of Individual Teachers

Some ineffective principals criticized individual teachers publicly, both indirectly and directly:

If our principal is angry or disagrees with a teacher, she will voice her negative thoughts in public to *other teachers*. This doesn't directly affect classroom teaching, but it does bring down school morale.

He has made negative comments about classroom noise, not to me privately but in the *presence of my students*.

This happened to a friend of mine. There were a lot of rumors going around about this teacher's performance—coming in late, not being professional, not fulfilling all teaching duties. Instead of dealing with this teacher privately and in a professional manner, the principal *talked to other teachers* about that person's performance before she talked to the teacher. This made the *rumors* intensify.

He *picks on* one teacher publicly in particular. He seems very biased against her. It hurts the morale of the school. She is an outstanding teacher, and he doesn't give her proper credit.

A past principal I had was *coercive* and *threatening*. She called out teachers' names in faculty meetings and used them as examples of what *not* to do. She threatened to move teachers to the temporary buildings if they did not conform to her ways.

Principals' Goals Related to Public Criticism

Teachers linked several control-oriented goals with ineffective principals' public criticism of them (e.g., exerting authority), but demonstrations of *power* were reported most often: "His goal is to show who is in control." Other goals were to "force" teachers to *resign* and to *correct* perceived wrongdoings: "to identify what she does not like in your actions."

Effects of Public Criticism

Not surprisingly, we learned that public criticism had a range of negative effects on teacher *motivation, self-esteem, morale,* and *trust and respect* for the principal. Significant increases in teacher *anger, avoidance, ignoring, resistance/rebellion,* and *cautiousness* were also apparent.

Public criticism also directly *interfered with teachers' routine instructional behavior.* To illustrate:

> [After she criticized teachers], I *hated* her. I worked to *undermine* her every move. The whole staff left. It is the wrong way to lead a school.

> I think the principal is thoughtless and not very aware of how he makes children and teachers nervous. It makes me *nervous* and *unsure* of myself. He creates a very *threatening* environment that is unnecessary. He likes making others *jump* so he has power.

> I thought that his remarks were *unprofessional* and *degrading*. I *avoided* all contact with him.

Public Criticism of Groups of Teachers: Shotgunning

Shotgunning refers to public criticism of a *group* of teachers—usually an entire faculty—when the conduct of particular teachers is at issue. Most frequently, such criticism of faculty took place at meetings:

> The principal frequently stands up in front of the *whole school* and tells us all the things we are doing wrong and that we are not doing our jobs. At times he names the people that he feels are not doing their jobs.

> My principal at times will come down on the faculty as a whole during a *faculty meeting*. It may be that certain teachers are not turning in their lesson plans on time or following through on a rule as cited in the handbook. This usually involves only a *handful* of teachers.

> He uses the shotgun approach at *faculty meetings*. Presumably a few teachers are doing something wrong, and the whole staff gets *preached* to.

Principals also used the intercom to criticize groups of faculty members:

She *announces* on the intercom a problem that one or two teachers are having and then *reprimands everyone* about it.

Principals used memoranda to publicly criticize teachers:

She sends out a *general memo* threatening to use the PDP or the GTEP [state evaluation] on *everyone* if the actions of certain individuals are not corrected.

We receive *memos* with an extremely negative tone. For example, in one the principal threatened us about the phone bill. He said, "Who has been making these calls? They will be traced." He issued this in the middle of the day and interrupted our classes to deliver it.

My principal issues *blanket reprimands* in faculty meetings, in newsletters, and in memos about poor punctuality, lack of time on task, record keeping, etc., rather than dealing with individuals. Evaluation is used to threaten all of us if problems are not taken care of.

Principals' Goals Related to Shotgunning

Most frequently, principals' goals included *demonstration of power* ("to remind us who is boss," "She likes to intimidate"), *control* ("She wants us to follow her dictates regarding meetings and duty schedules"), and less frequently, *efficiency* ("to take care of the problem with as little effort as possible") and *avoidance of conflict* ("to get the few to change without having to talk to them").

Effects of Public Criticism of Groups

Public criticism of groups produced strong negative effects on teacher *motivation, anger, respect* for principals, and *attention paid to* the principal. Teachers wrote,

"Chewing out" the whole staff when only a few are involved—it only makes me *angry*. I *ignore* remarks and suggestions and make no desired changes.

It makes me, as well as others, *angry* and *paranoid*. It makes me *watch* around corners.

I *resent* being grouped with teachers who are not fulfilling their responsibilities when I am doing my best to do so. Those to whom she is directing her remarks will probably not change until addressed directly, while other teachers will be *offended*.

He is scared to face the problem one-on-one. I hate this approach. It is *gutless*. Be a leader and do the job! I *lose respect* for anyone that uses the shotgun approach when the problem is clearly one or two already-identified individuals.

It's depressing. I think, "Is she preaching to me?" This diminishes my respect for her. Less than 100% of my energy will be devoted to teaching. Some of my *energy is lost* to negative feelings.

It's unfair to criticize everyone for what only a few do. I tend to *disregard* the importance of meetings because of this. It's very negative.

I don't think it's fair. I *resent* being threatened about a task I am already doing. Besides, it makes me wonder if the principal has discussed the problem with the individuals responsible. What is *he* doing if there is no improvement?

The principal frequently lists the things we are doing wrong. It makes me feel as though no matter what I do, it's not good enough. I *hate* it.

It makes me *wonder* if she's even aware of what's happening in the school. I wonder if she knows who is working with her to help the school run smoothly. Most people who are following the procedures are *resentful* of having to listen, time after time, to how things should be done. The ones who need the help may not hear her at all. It's *frustrating*.

I always wonder if she talks about me. Am I being targeted? I look at others and roll my eyes or say *negative* things about school morale. She's afraid to deal with teachers. I feel less professional, more like a tall child. This is one of those strategies I will never use when I am in a leadership position. I will deal with faculty problems on an individual basis.

As polar opposites, praise and criticism might be considered the good and the bad sides of leadership; as we have seen, one inspires, the other destroys. Regarding criticism, we note that seldom have the actions of principals been linked to such destructive effects on teachers. Our next chapter expands our comparisons of divergent leader behaviors and focuses on *extending autonomy* and *maintaining control*.

Extending Autonomy
Versus Maintaining Control

This is the third and final chapter in which we juxtapose two principal behaviors vis-à-vis classroom instruction: *extending autonomy* to teachers versus *maintaining control* of teachers. Also described are the effects these actions had on teachers and the goals principals pursued. We shall see, once again, that principals' actions have powerful consequences for teachers.

Extending Autonomy

Good principals frequently extended autonomy to teachers with regard to decisions about *instruction* (e.g., the "how" of teaching) as well as *program* development (e.g., content and instructional methods for subject areas and grade levels, or the "what" of teaching). Notably, our data indicate that extending autonomy is based on principals' confidence and trust in teachers' professional judgment:

> My principal treats me as a *professional.* I do not need to sign in or out, turn in lesson plans every week, etc. She assumes that we are in our rooms on time, teaching from bell to bell, and are fully prepared.

> In our school you have the *freedom to try* new things or experiment without being scrutinized. The teachers are given the *power* over

the curriculum. You can teach using your own expertise. I have written and teach my own personal physical education program.

She gives all teachers the *choice* to use whichever instructional approach we feel will best meet our children's highest potential.

My principal has enough confidence in me that she pretty much lets me teach *what I want.* The *style* of teaching I use is also up to me. She is concerned only with teaching what I have put on the student's IEP and in the lesson plans.

He acknowledges my expertise in my field of teaching and allows me the *freedom* to do what I feel is best in teaching that subject.

Why Is He or She Extending Autonomy?

According to our data, good principals extend autonomy to *motivate* teachers ("to encourage independence and flexibility and allow the teachers to do their level best," "to do the best job teachers can") and to *encourage innovation* in instruction. Clearly, by extending autonomy good principals recognize the importance of respecting teacher and student differences and allowing for the "teacher's interpretation of various goals for "specific kids and specific classrooms":

She recognizes that teachers are different, just like all learners are *different.* The principal wants teachers to use their best-educated guess as to the needs of the learners.

The goal is for me to teach new techniques and ideas to the *population* of students I work with.

The Effects of Encouraging Autonomy

Teachers reported that encouraging autonomy positively affected their *motivation, self-esteem, confidence,* professional *discretion,* sense of *security, reflection,* and *reflectively informed behavior.* However, it should be mentioned that the effects of extending autonomy on classroom instruction were not as robust as the effects of more direct principal approaches, such as giving postconference feedback and suggestions. (See Chapter 4 for more on reflection.)

This strategy reinforces my feelings of *esteem*. I feel more open to sharing my knowledge with other teachers and parents, and this motivates me to do the best job I can.

I love teaching with a whole language approach, and having the *freedom* to do so is wonderful.

My principal lets teachers instruct without interference from him. I feel more *confident* and more at ease to carry out lessons in the manner I see fit.

He allows teachers great freedom. This creates a very relaxed atmosphere and makes me *excited* about teaching. I am free to adjust teaching to individual needs. I willingly implement new materials and techniques, and I study to stay abreast of recent developments. I am constantly searching for ways to improve student performance. I think this strategy is extremely motivational for a self-motivated teacher.

Having autonomy allows me to develop and *grow* in my field. My supervisor allows me to implement new programs and to teach new techniques and ideas to the population of students I work with. I set higher goals for myself. She believes in my views and ideas.

I love the freedom of decision making for the classroom. I set *high expectations* for the students and design the workload to match. I don't care to have someone breathing down my neck.

We decide together what strategies or tactics to use for instruction. This is good because pressure would interfere with *creativity*.

Independence and flexibility allow the teachers to do their level best. I have the *independence* to follow my own teaching method and strategies. I am in a relaxed atmosphere, and this helps me to accomplish my teaching goals.

Autonomy makes me feel *respected*. I do not feel the pressure of someone always looking over my shoulder so I put more time and energy into my work. I look for new methods and techniques that stimulate students' learning. Her professional respect for me *motivates* me to always do this.

Some Negative Effects of Teacher Autonomy

Several teachers reported that although autonomy was useful to them, they felt that some teachers required closer (more directive) supervision:

> I feel that this strategy is good and bad. Good because teachers who are doing a good job have the *freedom* to carry out their plans effectively. It's bad because teachers who are not doing a good job are not being properly *monitored*.

In addition, a few teachers disclosed that they needed individual recognition for their work, and encouraging autonomy, in their cases, meant that they did not receive such recognition from the principal. (This would tend to be true, of course, only if principals failed to employ other effective instructional leadership strategies.)

The Control Orientation and Instructional Leadership

On the negative side, what we refer to as the control (dictatorial, authoritarian) orientation emerged strongly in our study as a dimension of ineffective instructional leadership. This orientation consists of several behaviors, including (1) *limiting teacher involvement in decision making*, (2) *unilaterally directing* a wide range of instructional aspects of teachers' work, and (3) *manipulating* teachers to control classroom instruction.

The control orientation, in general, had unfortunate negative impacts on teachers. Among others, controlling leadership had serious effects on teacher *reflection and reflectively informed* behavior. We observed other strong negative effects on teachers in the following areas:

- Motivation
- Anger
- Self-esteem

- Fearfulness
- Confusion
- Loss of respect and trust for the principal
- Thoughts of quitting teaching
- Compliance
- Avoidance
- Resistance/rebellion
- Quitting
- Lack of communication with the principal

Three Typical Behavior Patterns

Limiting Teacher Involvement in Decision Making

Authoritarian principals *limited teacher involvement in decision making* in many ways, for instance:

She *doesn't listen* or give you time to *voice* your opinion.

He would *not allow any group decisions* to be made on anything about instruction in my area.

My principal *shoots down* all ideas from teachers. I think, "What can I do to beat the system?" I want what is best for my kids. I feel *browbeaten.* I often feel I'm dealing underhandedly with the situation, but my head says I should do what's best for the kids, with or without the principal's support.

He *ignores* group decisions that might be difficult to enact but best for students.

He says, "I am the boss! I make the final decision."

She doesn't allow an atmosphere of dialogue and thinking.

Unilaterally Directing Instruction

A host of examples of principals' *unreasonable expectations linked to unilaterally directing* many aspects of teachers' classroom *instruction* were also found in our data set. We include many of these to illuminate their *dramatic negative effects* on teachers including effects on reflection and reflectively informed behavior.

> Our principal seems to *control every aspect* of instruction. After several years of being told how instruction was to be planned, delivered, and evaluated, I wasn't sure that I had a mind of my own. Her expectations were unrealistic, but I *conformed* because I had to survive. *Stress* was so strong and *fear* followed me through each day, but somehow I managed to *bury* myself in my students' needs, interests, and love, and we experienced success. Still, I know that I have to make some changes. How I wish I had the courage to go "outside the lines"!

> She was stern and controlling. She would *monitor* the halls, students, and classes. It was almost like she was *patrolling,* looking for the negative.

> My previous principal *spied* on me—listened on the intercom, dropped in unannounced, and sat down taking notes. He put "see me" *notes* in my box and usually asked for *meetings* on Friday afternoon or the day before vacations. At one point I was the only teacher in the school who was *not allowed* to get coffee or go to the restroom. I was always *fearful* of losing my job. I did *not* feel that I could *trust* any of my colleagues, and I was very isolated. I had no one to talk to. I began to doubt everything, and my *teaching suffered.* I had no administrative support. My relations with students, parents, colleagues, and family *suffered.* My husband got to the point that he wouldn't listen to me. This principal wanted to *destroy* me, and he almost succeeded. Then I transferred to a new school. A positive aspect of his lack of leadership is that *it inspired me to get into leadership.*

> In my first year of teaching, my principal required me to *memorize* the Teacher's Edition [of the reading text] and then gave me a test on the material. He also asked me to *account* for nearly every minute I was out of the classroom. I *despised* him, and I *dreaded* going to work every day. I had *no motivation,* never worked overtime, and called in sick a lot. One day, I *left the job in the middle of the day* and never returned.

My supervisor was *not flexible*! I like to bring in information related to science that is not part of the curriculum because I don't believe science is fun unless you relate it to current topics in the news or students' lives. But he was too *"by the book."* He wanted to make sure all of the science teachers were covering the same material. I had to be careful with extra materials, and I resented this. So I was a little *subversive*: I trained students to bring up the topics so I would just be answering their questions.

She tries to *force* us to complete a lesson in 45 minutes. She believes we should stay on schedule and devote equal time to all subjects. This *dilutes* the integration of reading, writing, and reasoning. It makes me think of ways I can *circumvent* her policies and integrate my teaching in a meaningful manner. I try to cram as much information as possible into 45 minutes. I feel pressed. I do not agree with her goals. I do not see how compartmentalizing subjects and using drill and practice will help with reasoning skills.

In the past, I worked with a principal who was unable to allow teachers to develop ideas. He had the need to *control* everything in the building. Teachers were told what to teach and how to teach it. The teacher became a *robotic extension* of the principal. Creativity was seen as subversive.

He *calls everyone* to a general inservice covering an issue some of us have already been exposed to and do not need to go over again. I always bring something else to *read* or do during the meeting.

He *decides* what inservice teachers should have and then gets upset when teachers aren't excited about the experiences. I *resent* being expected to implement something I don't believe in. I don't put forward my best effort. I don't have *ownership*.

I teach in a school that is 99% black students. I am a white male. My principal *directed* me to attend a conference entitled, "Young Black Men, the New Bold Eagles." At the conference, the critical message I received was that the problem was white men, and there is a conspiracy to destroy young black males. At the end of the session, I asked one of the presenters what to do. His platitudes were of no help, and I left the conference having heard that

I was the problem and could not be part of the solution. My principal was very *controlling* of his staff, and negative incidents like this simply confirmed his lack of respect for his staff.

She gets projects started with your name registered by her as the person responsible. Then she turns the project over to you in *midstream* without prior warning.

My principal will *not allow* me to carry out activities and to teach as suggested by the director of the Title I program. I cannot talk to the principal, so I am on the phone often with the Title I director. To keep the peace, I go ahead with *what I'm told* by the principal; my job is stressful enough without having her upset with me because I fail to follow her directions. I *resent* being told that county directors do not realize that things are different at our school. I feel that I am not being given a chance to teach and do justice to the children that I am serving. Often I am forced to *cancel* my scheduled classes because the principal wants me to do spur-of-the-moment work for her.

He uses the *"you will do this"* method. This may work in the military or if you have total trust in the dictator's judgment, but teachers, by nature, examine ideas and the structure of ideas. They feel the need to question the viability of a plan. They also know that not all plans work for all cases. What may work one time will not work another. I believe he does not like to discuss his plans because he has a unidimensional understanding of whatever it is he asks us to do and it will not hold up to scrutiny. He does not have a good understanding of instructional concepts, and I *rebel*. It's frustrating, *angering*. He's wrong. Even when he proves right, I have lost trust and believe he is wrong. I will *drag* my feet or not make changes in an effective manner.

Manipulating Teachers

Several teachers reported that principals employed manipulation to control them in the classroom. For example, teachers indicated that some principals used *guilt* to influence them: "She has a tendency to use the guilt trip on me. She tries to make you feel you are letting her down by any action or discussion she may feel opposed to." Contrived niceness was also experienced as manipulative by some teachers: "He is very nice when he needs something from our department but too busy when we need his input." "He attempts to be very friendly and informal when asking me to do things; he is trying to take advantage of my willingness to be a team player."

A few teachers pointed out that principals made disingenuous allusions to *professional knowledge* to manipulate them: "He refers to research to lead us to believe that we need to improve. Some of his comments are ridiculous though and aren't research based, are not proven theory. I can see through what he's doing." One teacher disclosed that her principal used *"blackmail"* to induce her to "spy on staff members."

Manipulation resulted in teachers' *loss of trust* for the principal. For some, it increased their *compliance,* and for others, it increased their *resistance*:

> I try to avoid certain subjects and I stay away from her. Other times, I don't want to hurt her feelings so I *go along* with her and just hope that others will voice their opinions.

> I *distrust* other faculty. I'm careful because they may talk to the principal. I have *stopped sharing* my ideas with the principal because he takes them as his own.

Other Aspects of Control

Some teachers indicated that although their principals purported to use a "shared governance" approach to leadership, the principals were, in reality, quite authoritarian and were interested in conveying only the image of shared decision making:

> I don't know if our principal trusts her staff. She *states* that we have ownership and she delegates authority, but she always does it her way anyway. This *turns* most teachers *off.* I feel like she thinks she's better than me, when in many instances all she has on me is a higher degree. I will still *jump through the hoops* because I know that's expected, but I'm *angry* and *hurt* that she doesn't put a lot of trust in her staff when she says she does.

Certain teachers explained that their principal's control orientation *varied* from day to day because of changes in mood:

> Sometimes she's OK, sometimes she's not. We *fear her moods.* We come to work not knowing if she'll misuse power—boss us around—or not. I fear her moods, but I *keep to myself* and always try to do the right thing, cover all the bases. She is the authority figure.

Shockingly, some principals were routinely *abusive* in their attempts to control teachers:

> She often *loses her temper* and *yells* at the staff. She gives ultimatums to control the staff.

> He tries to maintain absolute control through *threats, yelling, shouting, commands,* and *lies.* He *avoids* interacting with anyone, due to his ignorance regarding educational issues.

Goals of Principals' Control Orientation

Teachers identified several goals related to ineffective principals' control orientation to classroom instruction. Not surprisingly, principals' goals were most frequently described as seeking teacher *compliance.* Teachers gave the following examples:

- "Control to have the highest test scores"
- "Make teachers follow procedures"
- "Keep teachers informed of the principal's personal agenda"
- "Improve teacher effectiveness, whether needed or not"
- "Get everyone using his teaching techniques in classrooms"
- "Coerce teachers into doing what he wanted done and how he wanted it done"
- "Get her way no matter what the consequences"
- "Get me to participate in inservice or coursework that makes him look good to his superiors"

Teachers also stated that *maintaining the status quo, "keeping things static,"* was a goal of principals who used control strategies to influence classroom instruction:

> She wants to maintain the *status quo,* to do things the way they are always done, or for the easiest solution.

> He's not afraid to use his age and experience to try to coerce me into submission. I feel I'm wasting my time to put up with this. It makes me think twice before I approach him with innovative techniques or ideas. He's trying to keep me from *rocking the boat.* To be honest, it makes me think about quitting.

Demonstrating power was seen as another prominent goal of principals who employed control strategies:

> Teachers began to feel that perhaps they needed this dictatorial/dominant leadership because their self-confidence was damaged. Lessons became rote. Children were not challenged. *Negativity* became the norm. His need for dominance hurt the school. He was eventually moved when it became evident that the strong teachers were leaving the school year after year.

> She wants to destroy me.

> He was a controlling person. He got a charge out of intimidating us. He wants to exercise power. He wants obedient followers.

> . . . to show that she is the authority figure.

Less frequently, teachers identified principal control with attempts to satisfy and/or protect themselves from *external groups:*

> I can only suppose that she wants to keep all faculty under her control not so much because she feels responsible for teaching but because she is *intimidated* by outsiders.

> He tries to achieve continuity among teachers to get *angry parents* off his back.

He does this to satisfy community leaders.

A few teachers reported that *efficiency* was a goal of controlling principals: "He used dictatorial edicts for expediency." Finally, several teachers indicated that their principals' goals in using control were *unknown,* but ventured guesses as to what they were:

> I really don't know what his goal is. Maybe he acts this way due to a *lack of leadership skill* and training.

> I don't know. I think she actually wants to delegate but is *afraid* the results won't be what she wants.

Effects of Control

The remarks of several teachers illustrate some of the negative effects of principal control:

> My principal *ordered* us to use ITBS practice tests to improve test scores. It made me very negative and *resistant,* but I used the tests as ordered.

> Our principal tells us all we need to know; all decisions come from him, and some have not been thought out. He used positive behaviors only to *keep us quiet, to intimidate us into doing what he wanted.* I was quiet but did not base my work in the classroom on his decisions alone. I finally changed jobs because I found him *chauvinistic and limiting.*

> She wanted to make sure that all of the science teachers were doing the *same* thing and covering the same material.

The Abusive Control Orientation:
The Worst of All

We have seen that extending autonomy tends to be beneficial to teachers and that in general principals' controlling behaviors tend to have adverse effects on teachers and their performance. What follows is a sampling of ineffective principals' actions that border on the *ugly*. Indeed, some principals exhibited behaviors that were disrespectful and occasionally even *destructive* to teachers' very souls. We believe that such behaviors must be avoided at all costs. Read the accounts below—including teachers' bitter reactions—and you will see the frustration, contempt, and hatred bred by principals' abusive, control-oriented behaviors.

My principal tries to tell me that an effective teacher is the one who has strict control of the students. She likes my class to be *rigid*: no movement by any child, and they speak only when spoken to, as if they are in the military. But I teach advanced classes, and sometimes I need to let them socialize or debate over certain issues without intervening. *I don't feel comfortable* talking to her about how I feel about her strategy because she hardly ever laughs and is always judgmental.

His goal was to gather and maintain power. I revolted or mutinied. Every chance I got, I would try to *gain more power* at his expense. I *hated* this person and I wanted to get even.

She tries to push her ideas off on me, not really giving me a choice. I hate to talk with her because it is *pointless* anyway. I try to *avoid* her at all costs. I don't like being pushed around, but I can be persuaded if it is for the good of everyone involved. And I have to consider what she wants if I am to maintain my job.

She dictates what the class schedule will be, and it ticks me off! I am forced to teach a subject I don't like, and so I don't give 100%. I am powerless to change the school. I *hate* her stance that no teachers have better ideas than she does. She ought to try other ideas . . . but she's so *closed-minded*!

His *refusal to listen* to teachers makes me feel that my input isn't important and my teaching expertise is *not valued*. This makes me less willing to make any extra effort to do new things. It's frustrating!

He often pressures teachers to do like he wants them to do; therefore, you don't feel like you want to give your best! I feel like I have been *stuffed in a bottle and have no air to breathe*. I go along with what is expected because I have been raised to do that, but I have a deep *resentment* and I brood about it.

He uses authoritarian power to tell us what to teach and how to teach. He's too *overbearing* about things he really doesn't understand. I *do my own thing* behind closed doors. Even his approval demeans my professionalism. I know what's best for my first graders. His approach makes me angry. I feel *worthless* because my ideas as a teacher don't matter.

He is an *idiot*. When he uses his position to enforce his will, it creates a fear of failure. Now I am less inspired. Needless to say, I *hate* it!

Sometimes I feel *incapable and weak* because I am really a touchy-feely person.

Sometimes I feel *unappreciated,* like she doesn't take the time to see how much I really do to meet the needs of all my kids. I prefer to feel inspired rather than *afraid.* I feel resentful instead of full of admiration. I, like other staff members, *don't put forth* the extra effort required.

She made decisions about learning improvement plans for students without consulting the staff. I felt like I was being "done to." There was no *ownership* by the staff.

I don't like being *treated like a child*! I should have some input. I get angry, and that can alter my mood and thoughts for my class. My behavior exhibits that. I want input!

My principal was concerned only with maintaining quiet classrooms. If I had to work with this principal too long, I would have *gotten out* of education. I had a very structured class with very little interaction among students. Aside from some peer tutoring, I almost always *lectured* and then gave an assignment. Sometimes I'm amazed I lasted for those two years and that I'm still in education.

Our principal is set in her thinking: Her way is the *only way.* We feel that what we have to say is secondary or really not up to par with her expectations. After I jokingly recommended to her to lighten up, she quickly put me in my place and reminded me that all teachers and administrators had a big job to do. I too am a professional, and I don't need her to tell me what to do. She has, I'm sure, read the book *How to Win Friends and Influence People*, but I don't think she'll ever get the message because she thinks she is perfect and really has nothing else to learn. How sad. She will *tell* you she is open to new ideas, but I know for a fact that is a *joke*!

I believe that my supervisor is unreasonable because she speaks no foreign languages but insists on telling me how I should instruct my foreign language students. But I continue to teach the class as I see fit, unless my supervisor is present. She is *unfair*, *unjust*, and *ineffective*.

She is a *micromanager*; I am constantly being *watched*. I have to run things by her before doing them. She is very *frustrating* because you have to wait until you get her approval. There's constantly the feeling of someone looking over you.

He told me I would teach a certain class and coach cheerleading *or else*. I had disbelief at first. The man's a total [expletive]! I wanted to *get out* of teaching altogether. I *despised* him and I felt betrayed. I did enough *to get by*, but then I realized that wasn't fair for the sake of my students whom I adored. So I went to the other extreme and, in spite of this man, did my very best with my teaching. I began trying new strategies and new ideas.

Summary

This chapter and the two preceding ones portray the good and bad behaviors that powerfully influence teachers and their instruction. Clearly, principal visibility (wandering around), praise, and support for teacher autonomy are the healthy counterpoint to principal interruption and abandonment, criticism, and authoritarian control. The final chapter presents our view of instructional leadership, with its potential for professional growth as well as its challenges.

Conclusion:
Building a Learning Community

[Supervision is] a way to assist and facilitate the professional activities of teachers working collaboratively to achieve school improvement through shared decision making.

Zepeda, Wood, & O'Hair, 1996, p. 29

The goal in a learning community is to build connections between people, socially and intellectually. Control interferes with this process; it distances people from one another. Commitment strengthens interpersonal connections. As I have argued elsewhere, building a learning community is tantamount to developing a commitment to shared learning.

Prawat, 1993, p. 9

In this book we have described principals' good instructional leadership and its coordinate behaviors and goals. More specifically, using the teachers' own words, we have presented descriptions of three *primary elements* of good instructional leadership that emerged in our study:

- Conducting instructional conferences
- Providing staff development
- Developing teacher reflection

Findings related to good principals' use of visibility, praise, and autonomy—juxtaposed with ineffective principals' use of abandonment, criticism, and control—were also presented.

We explicated each of the three primary elements of good instructional leadership by discussing our findings in relation to other relevant research. For example, our data indicated that the element of *conducting conferences* with teachers included such behaviors as making suggestions, giving feedback, modeling, using inquiry, and soliciting advice and opinions from teachers. We discussed this element of instructional leadership in the context of other research that describes principals' use of a developmental approach, a variety of data-gathering procedures, and appropriate conference types vis-à-vis a teacher's needs and goals.

Behaviors associated with *providing staff development* included emphasizing the study of teaching and learning, support for collaboration, development of coaching relationships, use of action research, provision of resources, and application of the principles of adult growth and development to all phases of the staff development program.

Another element, *developing teacher reflection*, included behaviors such as modeling, classroom observation, dialogue, suggestion, and praise. The essence of reflection, as we found, was associated with collegial inquiry, critical thinking, and expanding teaching repertoires.

Why were these behaviors effective with teachers? According to our data, principals' use of these behaviors had "enhancing" *affective, cognitive,* and *behavioral* effects on teachers. In other words, they dramatically and positively impacted teachers' feelings and attitudes, thinking, and instructional behavior.

Theoretically speaking, our data suggest that these three types of effects tended to interact with one another. For example, effects on motivation and self-esteem prompted reflection, and this tended to result in greater reflectively informed behavior in the classroom. Clearly, effective instructional leadership by school principals tends to affect teachers holistically, that is, emotionally, intellectually, and behaviorally.

Conversely, according to our study, principals' use of single behaviors *only*, for example, distributing the professional literature to teachers—a behavior that only provides information about a new teaching technique but does not affect teachers emotionally—was disproportionately less influential in affecting teacher reflection and reflectively informed behavior. Stated differently, principal instructional leadership that results in positive feelings *and* provides teachers with relevant, concrete information to improve instruction will most likely result in greater reflectively informed classroom behavior.

Other reasons for the effectiveness of the principal behaviors identified above are related to the fact that these behaviors accomplish the following:

1. *Give teachers choice and discretion.* Teachers were not typically required by principals to implement a suggestion; they were asked to "consider" suggestions and then given the opportunity to choose their own path.

2. *Foster nonthreatening interaction.* Interactions between teachers and principals were not based on direct and overt critique of the teacher's teaching; rather, interactions were growth oriented, supportive, and positive. The core of such interactions was expanding teachers' strengths instead of focusing on minor deficits.

3. *Provide evidence of authentic interest.* Principals' positive behaviors reflected true caring and interest in the teacher's professional growth. For instance, giving suggestions was seen as an expression of wanting to help and support teachers, and praise was seen as believable, authentic, and based on concrete data.

4. *Allow for "pleasing the principal."* In some cases, principals influenced teachers because teachers felt obligated or motivated to please the principal. Usually this was based on respect for or appreciation of the principal's approach to leadership, so teachers allowed themselves to be influenced by the strategy.

It should be reemphasized that although praise had positive effects on teacher reflection and reflectively oriented behavior, most of the teachers in our study who discussed praise specifically identified major effects on esteem and good feelings in general. At the same time, we found that when praise was used along with substantive principal behaviors, it tended to enhance the effects of these behaviors.

In each chapter we have described those elements and behaviors that *emerged directly from our data*. Thus, the portrait of a good instructional leader presented in this book was drawn entirely from data produced by teachers working in typical U.S. schools. These data argue that teachers' classroom instruction can be significantly enhanced by powerful instructional leadership behaviors—often enacted as supervision—by principals. To date, no empirical research has been published focusing on the behaviors that principals who are considered good instructional leaders use and the specific effects of such behaviors on teachers' affective states, cognition regarding teaching and learning, and instructional behavior.

What, Then, Is Good Instructional Leadership or Supervision?

In discussing the furor in the field of instructional supervision in recent years (including debates, publications, conference proceedings, and other professional dialogue), Zepeda et al. (1996) conclude that, in the near future, emerging trends in supervisory practice will emphasize the following:

1. *Training for administrators as well as teachers* in supervision, mentoring, and coaching
2. Sensitivity to the processes of professional *growth* and continuous *improvement*
3. *Training in observation and reflection on practice* in teacher preparation programs
4. *Integration* of supervision with staff development, curriculum development, and school improvement systems
5. *Improved professional practice* both in and outside the classroom
6. *Continuous improvement* as part of every educator's daily life
7. *Focus on group processes* in classrooms rather than a one-on-one supervisory experience
8. *Collegial assistance* among educators, parents, and students

9. Use of terms such as *colleague consultation* and *coaching* to describe collaboration among professionals helping each other to improve practice

These emerging trends are consistent with what appeared in our study as good principal instructional leadership. In addition, we recommend greater use of "autosupervision," that is, teachers' supervision of their own instructional practices including self-analysis, reflectivity, monitoring one's own progress toward goals, and implementing changes based on reflection. Unquestionably, some teachers are capable of, comfortable with, and even prefer such an approach to professional growth. More research in this aspect of supervision would be valuable.

In essence, our findings confirm that good supervisory practice should no longer emphasize *control and competition* among teachers: The prevalent negative associations that derive from "control supervision" simply must give way to various forms of collegiality among educators. Supervision should avoid restrictive and intimidating approaches to teachers, as well as approaches that provoke little more than teachers "jumping through hoops" and giving "dog and pony shows" based on reductionist algorithms presumed to define good teaching in their classrooms. Instead, supervision should work toward the development of professional *dialogue* among educators. We recommend that to expand as a viable influence on teacher classroom instruction, supervision (or instructional leadership) should embrace efforts such as those listed below:

- Coordination of *one-to-one assistance* programs among teachers
- *Schoolwide efforts* to improve teaching and learning
- Implementation of *parent-teacher partnerships* for classroom observation and interpretation of student behaviors
- Development of *action research* programs to inform decision making
- Initiation of *collegial study groups* to share successes, problems, research, and dialogue about teaching and learning
- Development of *mentoring* programs
- *The teaching of teaching*, with sharing of results with other teachers

- Use of a variety of *self-assessment and self-improvement* plans
- *Reflective* discussion and writing (logs, journals, biography) by educators (see Gordon, 1997, for more examples)

By no means, however, are we recommending that supervision become entirely nondirective. Indeed, for some teachers in some circumstances (e.g., an overwhelmed preservice teacher, a weak teacher, or a teacher with less acute analytical skills), a prescriptive approach may be warranted.

The "disharmonious condition of the field of educational supervision may signal a gloomy outlook" (Glanz, 1997c, p. 203), particularly in light of the field's autocratic legacy (an issue we discussed earlier). However, Glanz sees the present state of affairs as an opportunity and recommends adopting the *Taoist perspective*. This approach embraces diversity and the ambiguity of change so as to promote excellence and professional growth. For example, a Taoist would answer the following questions with a "yes":

- Is it possible that a *variety of theories* or conceptual frameworks can influence supervisory practice?
- Is it possible for supervisors, as middle-management personnel, to find ways of accepting inherent *ambiguities*?
- Is it possible to accept that supervision, as a process, can be carried out by *many different individuals* concerned with instructional improvement?
- Is it possible for supervisors to accept teachers as *partners* in instructional decision making?
- Is it possible that *evaluation and supervision* can be accomplished by one individual?
- Is it possible for supervisors to realize that their *invisibility* in the school organization may be their greatest asset?
- Is it possible that supervision, broadly reconceptualized, does not imply a blandness of purpose, but a *richness of diversity*?
- Is it possible to accept and employ a *variety of models* of supervision? (Glanz, 1997c, p. 210)

Relatedly, Sergiovanni (1997) referred to supervision as *pedagogical leadership*, as derived from van Mannen's (1991) concept of pedagogy as "a kind of 'leading' that often walks *behind* the one who is led" (Sergiovanni, 1997, p. 279). Sergiovanni also brilliantly defined a *community theory of leadership,* a pastoral supervision, which is covenantal, reflective, and care giving, as is found in the ministry. *Ministerial roles* of principals and other supervisors include the following:

1. *Purposing*—bringing together shared visions into a covenant that speaks compellingly to principals, teachers, parents, and students with a moral voice.

2. *Maintaining harmony*—building a consensual understanding of school purposes, of how the school should function, and of the moral connections between roles and responsibilities, while respecting individual conscience and individual style differences.

3. *Institutionalizing values*—translating the school's covenant into a workable set of procedures and structures that facilitates the accomplishment of school purposes and provides normative systems for directing and guiding behavior.

4. *Motivating*—providing for the basic psychological needs of members, on one hand, and for the basic cultural needs of members to experience sensible and meaningful school lives, on the other.

5. *Managing*—ensuring the necessary day-to-day support (such as planning, organizing, agenda setting, mobilizing resources, providing procedures, and record keeping) that keeps the school running effectively and efficiently.

6. *Explaining*—giving reasons for asking members to do certain things and giving explanations that link what they are doing to the larger picture.

7. *Enabling*—removing obstacles that prevent members from meeting their commitments on one hand and providing resources and support that help members to meet their commitments on the other.

8. *Modeling*—accepting responsibility as head follower of the school's covenant by modeling purposes and values in thought, word, and action.

9. *Supervising*—providing the necessary oversight to ensure that the school is meeting its commitments and, when it is not, to find out why and help everyone do something about it. (Sergiovanni, 1997, pp. 275-276)

The good principals described in our study performed many of the ministerial roles Sergiovanni describes. Specifically, our data demonstrate the harmonizing, valuing, enabling, and modeling roles of good instructional leaders, all of which comprise a rich and relevant base to promote the professional growth of teachers.

Good Leadership Vis-à-Vis Instruction

Our study expands the literature on the nature of principal influence, particularly on classroom instruction. Nevertheless, the effects of supervision on teacher behavior in general require further study. For example, Larsen and Malen (1997) described the fundamentally *political* nature of principal-teacher interactions. They raised questions about the *complexity* of leadership and influence, as well as the *conditions* in which political interactions occur. They concluded that principal influence on curriculum and instructional decision making may be contingent on a multitude of factors (e.g., one's goals, resources, motivations, strategies, and setting—that is, a district allowing building-level decision making).

We would argue that as supervision of instruction becomes more collaborative, collegial, and democratic (as suggested above), it will become increasingly political in terms of the (1) *frequency* of power and influence-based interactions between, for example, principals and teachers as well as (2) the *kinds* of political interactions that can be expected (e.g., debate) from all participants, based on greater trust and respect for professional knowledge.

We also note that in discussing school leadership in general, other theorists and researchers have suggested the following roles and behaviors for would-be educational leaders. (Consider how such roles would shape instructional leadership.)

- Administrators should be critical *humanists* who support the goals of democracy (Foster, 1986; Soder, 1995).

- School leaders should adopt the ethic of *caring*, thus encouraging schools to become nurturing communities for children of all races, classes, and genders (Noddings, 1986).

- Administrators should operate from their personal *values* (Giroux, 1992) and should *lead with soul, passion, and purpose* (Bolman & Deal, 1995).

- The heart of school improvement is *moral* leadership (Sergiovanni, 1996).

- Principals must acknowledge that good instruction rests on a base of human and social resources. Factors *essential* to promoting student achievement include leadership, parent involvement, professional commitment and collaboration among the staff, and an orientation toward learning standards and innovation (Consortium on Chicago School Research, 1996; Schlecty, 1997).

Tips for Principals

School renewal and support for teacher performance and growth should focus not only on solving specific problems through the use of innovations. Beyond this, there must be a "fluid inquiry" into possibilities that may include redesign of job assignments, democratic reorganization, study of data about the learning environment, sharing a professional knowledge base, new forms of staff development, and the creation of caring professional communities (Joyce & Calhoun, 1995). This radical work, set within a complicated technical, political, social, moral, and psychological milieu, must be led by special people, people who are determined and able to *build a learning community*:

> People who view themselves primarily as managers, as men or women of action, who "make things happen," who "shake things up—these people are ill equipped to play the role required of someone who builds a learning community. The person who builds a learning community might better be described as a child or adult "developmentalist," someone who knows where he or she stands on the issues; someone who has a well-developed theory of teaching and learning based on the best current work in education. This individual recognizes the need that others have

to construct understanding on their own. He or she is comfortable with the give and take of spirited discussion; this person understands the importance of striking a balance between support and challenge, between honoring each individual's contribution to the group while at the same time moving the group toward more powerful, disciplinary-based ways of viewing education phenomena. (Prawat, 1993, p. 9)

From our study of teachers who worked with good instructional leaders, we offer the following suggestions:

1. *Talk openly and frequently with teachers about instruction.* We have found that instructional leadership requires leaders with very different skills, knowledge, attitudes, and personal characteristics from those routinely taught and developed in educational leadership programs. Our research confirms that the new supervisor *talks* with teachers and discusses classroom activity with them. Glanz (1997b) has said,

> Notwithstanding the complex social, political, technological, and moral challenges confronting instructional leaders as we approach the new century, I think that the most critical issue before us remains finding ways to alter belief systems and to relieve the bureaucratic paralysis that encourages principals and other supervisors to rely on simplistic evaluative measures rather than engaging teachers meaningfully in instructional improvements. Seriously dialoguing with teachers about sound pedagogical practices and providing them, at their request, with verifiable information about what is going on in their classroom is what "good" instructional supervision is all about. Research indicates that teachers will likely change their instructional behaviors on their own, after their classrooms have been described to them, nonjudgmentally. (p. 6)

Furthermore, Cangelosi (1991) asserts that supervision includes analysis of teaching as a complex art. This requires a cooperative, nonthreatening teacher-supervisor partnership; such a partnership includes openness and freedom to make mistakes. Many teachers in our study described the open and trusting nature of relationships with their principals.

2. *Provide time and peer connections for teachers.* The good instructional leader also realizes that the mutuality of a collaborative process, rather than a single, authoritarian approach, elevates teachers as thoughtful, responsible, growing professionals. Thus, the leader not only works to develop structural conditions (e.g., time for collaborative planning and responsibility to make key decisions) but also attempts to develop core human and social resources (e.g., culture, climate, and interpersonal relationships) to enhance professional community in schools and to enact school improvement and reform (Louis, Marks, & Kruse, 1996).

Teachers in our study discussed their principals' willingness to grant much-needed *time* for instructional endeavors. In Raywid's (1993) view, time is central:

> If collaborative endeavor is necessary to school adequacy, then *schools* must provide it. The responsibility rests with schools, not individual teachers. Further, administrators, policymakers, and public alike must accept a new conception of school time. If we are to redefine teachers' responsibilities to include collaborative sessions with colleagues—and both organizational research and teacher effectiveness research now suggest they are essential to good schools—then it is necessary to reconstrue teacher time. The time necessary to examine, reflect on, amend, and redesign programs is not auxiliary to teaching responsibilities—nor is it "released time" from them. It is absolutely central to such responsibilities, and essential to making schools succeed! (p. 34)

More broadly, in terms of *peer connections*, Loup (1995) suggests enhancing several organizational features of schools to enable teachers to work together:

> Organizational effectiveness, although not sufficient, may be a necessary condition to increase school holding power (e.g., attendance) and productivity (i.e., student achievement). Thus, the first order of business for effective school leaders and for school improvement and change efforts may be to enhance school organizational effectiveness by measuring and altering various organizational features of schools (e.g., organizational coupling features, decision making structures, organizational/supervisory climate). (p. 31)

3. *Empower teachers.* Freire (1985) tells us that empowerment occurs within free, mutual, and critical dialogue, not in judgment and evaluation. The good instructional leaders we described clearly realized this, and we found ample evidence of empowerment of teachers as assessed by Short and Rinehart's (1992) School Participant Empowerment Scale, which measures the following:

- Decision making (responsibility, input, peer teaching)
- Professional growth (continued learning, collaboration)
- Status (respect, knowledge base, support)
- Autonomy (control, freedom)
- Impact (ability to get things done, influence, participation in staff development)
- Self-efficacy (helping kids learn, making a difference)

Self-efficacy, in particular, tends to be reinforced by three primary leadership behaviors: modeling, inspiring group purpose, and providing rewards. Several other behaviors contributed to self efficacy: promoting teacher empowerment, creating a positive climate, fostering teamwork and collaboration, encouraging innovation and continual growth, believing in staff and students, managing student behavior, and inspiring caring and respect (Blase & Blase, 1994; Blase & Blase, 1997; Hipp, 1995). *All* of these factors were evident, in varying degrees, in the study discussed in this book.

4. *Understand and embrace the challenges of change.* Many researchers have described the challenge and complexity of change in schools, especially schools in the throes of reform and restructuring. Some believe that teachers may be disinclined to examine their work critically. At the same time, other writings help us understand teachers' resistance to change. For example, resistance to change may be rooted in stereotyping or misunderstandings, the causes of which may be age-related phases, individual growth states, and age stereotyping (Rusch, 1993).

Indeed, Schmuck and Runkel (1994) have aptly shown how difficult change is, how all persons in a school must alter their role conceptions and behaviors in order to effect change. Fullan and Miles (1992) offer seven helpful propositions for successful change. (Can you identify those beliefs held by the principals we discussed?)

a. **Change is learning.** It is loaded with uncertainty and involves learning and risk taking.

b. **Change is a journey, not a blueprint.**

c. **Problems are our friends.** We should actively seek and confront real problems in order to make effective responses to complex situations.

d. **Change is resource-hungry.** It requires resources such as training, materials, time, and support.

e. **Change requires the power to manage it.** Leadership is essential.

f. **Change is systemic.** It must focus on developing all interrelated school components and culture.

g. **All large-scale change is implemented locally.** (pp. 749-752)

5. *Lead.* Little (1993) states that professional development emphasizes the "teacher as intellectual rather than teacher as technician" (p. 129). Thus, a principal's fundamental respect for the knowledge and abilities of teachers goes far in helping teachers develop themselves professionally. Indeed, even bureaucratically mandated forms of collegiality such as peer coaching may, over time, coupled with good school-based instructional leadership, produce increasingly positive attitudes toward professional growth in teachers. Wise principals balance *support and guidance* with *opportunity and leading from behind.* They are neither heavy-handed nor afraid to push gently in the right direction.

More to Learn

After completing the study that forms the basis of this book, we realized that our work is far from done. To be sure, the study of instructional leadership is but one tile—albeit a significant one—in the complex and ever-changing mosaic of leadership. We have not yet achieved a full understanding of myriad related issues such as adult growth, career development, reflective thinking, coaching, and power elements of interaction. Refreshingly, the continuing study of instructional leadership, partially illuminated by work such as this, is testament to the essence of all who work in our field, from teaching to leading: It is a matter of lifelong learning.

Resource:
Research Method and Procedures

This book has focused on the characteristics of school principals that effectively influence classroom instruction. For those readers who may be interested in reviewing the research method and procedures employed to produce the database for this book, we offer the following description:

Data collection and analysis were consistent with symbolic interaction theory. Although this approach acknowledges that structural factors influence human action, the meanings that people attribute to action are emphasized. In essence, people's reflexivity is given greater importance than structural factors. As a product of social action, the individual is influenced by others but also maintains sufficient distance from others and is capable of initiating individual action (Blumer, 1969; Mead, 1934). Symbolic interaction, in contrast to some qualitative research approaches, stresses individual perception and interpretation.

Accordingly, for the study reported in this book we used open-ended questions and investigated the broad questions, What characteristics (e.g., strategies, behaviors, attitudes, goals) of school principals positively influence classroom teaching, and conversely, what characteristics of school principals adversely affect classroom teaching? In both cases, we examined principals' actions (and lack of action) that influence classroom teaching from the teacher's perspective.

Consistent with exploratory-inductive approaches to qualitative inquiry, no a priori definitions of strategies were used to direct data

collection. Rather, we gathered data and analyzed these data to produce descriptive categories, themes, and conceptual and theoretical
understandings (Bogdan & Biklen, 1982; Bogdan & Taylor, 1975; Glaser,
1978; Glaser & Strauss, 1967).

Allport (1942) has argued that an open-ended questionnaire is
considered a personal document in qualitative research that examines
a person's subjective perspectives. Such a questionnaire is defined as
any self-revealing document that intentionally or unintentionally yields
information regarding the structure, dynamics, and functioning of the
author's life (p. xii). Accordingly, a questionnaire is a personal document when research participants have substantial control over the
content of their responses.

Although questionnaires like this have been used in much published
research recently, it should be mentioned that the study described in this
book focuses on teachers' perspectives of principal strategies. The consistency of teachers' perceptions, for example, in comparison with principals' perceptions, cannot be demonstrated in our study. In fact, symbolic interaction theory argues that the perspectives of others can be
expected to vary (Blumer, 1969; Bogdan & Taylor, 1975; Mead, 1934).

The Inventory of Strategies Used by Principals to Influence Classroom Teaching (ISUPICT), an open-ended questionnaire, was designed to collect personal meanings on the study topic. We developed
an initial version of the questionnaire in consultation with professors
and teachers. The instrument was pilot-tested with several university
classes of teachers who were graduate students at a major university
in the Southeastern United States. Suggestions made by these individuals were used to construct the final form of the inventory.

In addition to a cover page introducing the research topic on the
ISUPICT, we explained that several factors led us to think that principals'
characteristics may influence classroom teaching. We also stated that
despite these factors, respondents may not feel that their principal positively or negatively influences their teaching. Teachers were also asked
to give background information on the cover page of the inventory.

On two appended legal-size pages, teachers were asked to provide detailed descriptions of one *positive* characteristic (one that had a
positive impact on their classroom teaching) and one *negative* characteristic (or behavior/lack of action that had a negative impact on
classroom teaching). More than one principal could be discussed.
In addition, questions about how such characteristics *affect* teaching,
principal's *goals, effectiveness* of characteristics, and teacher's *feelings*

about characteristics are included. The questions listed on page 2 of the questionnaire are reproduced below (page 3 focuses on *negative* characteristics.)

1. Describe and give a detailed *example* of a *POSITIVE* characteristic (overt or covert; formal or informal) that your instructional supervisor uses frequently to influence what you think or do that directly improves something about your classroom teaching. (Please use other side of paper if necessary.)

2. Describe and give a real-life example of the *effect* (impact) that the characteristic has on your *thoughts (related to teaching) and behavior (related to teaching)*.

3. Describe and illustrate your instructional supervisor's *goals* associated with the characteristic you identified above.

4. How *effective* is the characteristic in getting you to *think* or *do* what the instructional supervisor intended?

   ineffective   effective

   |___|___|___|___|___|___|

   Please explain why:

5. What *feelings* do you have about the instructional supervisor's characteristic?

We administered the inventory to a total of 809 teachers taking graduate courses at three major state universities located in the Southeastern, Midwestern, and Northwestern United States. The study sample consisted of male ($n = 251$) and female ($n = 558$) teachers from rural ($n = 275$), suburban ($n = 291$), and urban ($n = 243$) schools. Elementary ($n = 380$), middle/junior ($n = 177$), and high school teachers ($n = 252$) participated. The average age of teachers was 37; the average number of years in teaching was 11. The sample included tenured ($n = 606$) and nontenured ($n = 203$) teachers. Married ($n = 598$) and single ($n = 211$) teachers participated. Degrees earned were B.A./B.S. ($n = 218$), M.Ed. ($n = 459$), Ed.S. ($n = 97$), and Ed.D./Ph.D. ($n = 35$). Teachers described both male ($n = 398$) and female ($n = 411$) principals. The mean number of years with the current principal at the time of this study was 4.

Given the open-ended nature of the ISUPICT, a period of about 35 minutes was required for its completion. Participation in this study was voluntary, and all questionnaires were completed anonymously.

Data from the study respondents were coded according to principles for inductive research and comparative analysis (Glaser, 1978; Glaser & Strauss, 1967). This form of analysis requires a comparison of each new unit of data with those coded previously for emergent categories and subcategories.

Each questionnaire page generated one principal characteristic (strategy, behavior, attitude, goal). (Each research participant was given two characteristic pages—one positive and one negative—to complete.) We further analyzed these data into several major positive characteristics and several major negative characteristics. Some negative data included behavior or lack of behavior (e.g., a failure to visit classrooms) not intentionally used by the principal.

Each characteristic was then analyzed to determine its impact on teachers' feelings, thinking, and behavior as these related to classroom teaching. Also analyzed were data generated by a 6-point scale to determine the ineffectiveness or effectiveness of each characteristic in influencing teachers. The mean effectiveness score for all positive characteristics was 5.4, and the mean effectiveness score for all negative strategies and behaviors or lack thereof was 2.6. (Note: A low effectiveness score does not mean that a negative characteristic such as authoritarianism or being critical had some positive impact on teachers. In most cases it simply meant that the characteristic had an impact of some perceived strength as far as teachers were concerned, usually in a negative direction.)

We designed display matrices to synthesize data for all positive and negative characteristics (Miles & Huberman, 1984). These matrices were used to identify and refine conceptual and theoretical ideas derived from the data. For example, such matrices permitted comparisons across the characteristics. This protocol also permitted comparisons of the descriptive and theoretical ideas produced by the study with the relevant extant literature (Glaser, 1978; Glaser & Strauss, 1967).

Two researchers analyzed the entire data set. Professors, doctoral students, and teachers were consulted on a regular basis when questions arose. To check the researchers' analysis, coders inspected segments of the research data. In brief, coders matched quotations drawn from the data with categories constructed by the researchers for both positive and negative characteristics and positive and negative impacts on teachers. The degree of consistency among raters was high (.90).

References

Acheson, K. A., & Gall, M. D. (1997). *Techniques in the clinical supervision of teachers: Preservice and inservice applications* (4th ed.). White Plains, NY: Longman.

Allport, G. (1942). *The use of personal documents in psychological science.* New York: Social Science Research Council.

Alrichter, H., & Posch, P. (1989). Does the grounded theory approach offer a guiding paradigm for teaching research? *Cambridge Journal of Education, 19*(1), 21-31.

Anderson, R. H. (1989). Unanswered questions about the effect of supervision on teacher behavior: A research agenda. *Journal of Curriculum and Supervision, 4*(4), 291-297.

Bates, R. (1984). Toward a critical practice of educational administration. In T. Sergiovanni & J. Corbally (Eds.), *Leadership and organizational culture* (pp. 240-259). Urbana and Chicago: University of Illinois Press.

Berliner, D. C. (1988). Implications of studies on expertise in pedagogy for teacher education and evaluation. In *New directions for teacher assessment* (proceedings of the 1988 ETS Invitational Conference, pp. 39-68). Princeton, NJ: Educational Testing Service.

Blase, J. (1993). The micropolitics of effective school-based leadership: Teachers' perspectives. *Educational Administration Quarterly, 29*(2), 142-163.

Blase, J., & Blase, J. R. (1994). *Empowering teachers: What successful principals do.* Thousand Oaks, CA: Corwin.

Blase, J., Blase, J. R., Anderson, G., & Dungan, S. (1995). *Democratic principals in action: Eight pioneers.* Thousand Oaks, CA: Corwin.

Blase, J. R. (1995). Supervision: Time for a name change? *Instructional Supervision Newsletter, 15*(1), 4-5.

Blase, J. R., & Blase, J. (1996). Micropolitical strategies used by administrators and teachers in instructional conferences. *Alberta Journal of Educational Research, 152*(4), 345-360.

Blase, J. R., & Blase, J. (1997). *The fire is back! Principals sharing school governance.* Thousand Oaks, CA: Corwin .

Blase, J., & Hekelman, F. (1996). Peering in on peers: The unexamined encounter. *Faculty Development News and Views, 9*(1), 4-6.

Blumberg, A. (1980). *Supervisors and teachers: A private cold war.* Berkeley, CA: McCutchan.

Blumberg, A., & Amidon, E. (1965). Teacher perceptions of supervisor-teacher interactions. *Administrator's Notebook, 14*(1), 1-4.

Blumberg, A., & Cusick, P. (1970). Supervisor-teacher interaction: An analysis of verbal behavior. *Education, 91,* 126-134.

Blumer, H. (1969). *Symbolic interactionism: Perspective and method.* Englewood Cliffs, NJ: Prentice Hall.

Bogdan, R., & Biklen, S. (1982). *Qualitative research for education: An introduction to theory and methods.* Boston: Allyn & Bacon.

Bogdan, R., & Taylor, S. (1975). *Introduction to qualitative research methods: A phenomenological approach to the social sciences.* New York: John Wiley.

Bolman, L. G., & Deal, T. E. (1991). *Reframing organizations: Artistry, choice, and leadership.* San Francisco: Jossey-Bass.

Bolman, L. G., & Deal, T. E. (1995). *Leading with soul.* San Francisco: Jossey-Bass.

Bolton, R. (1979). *People skills: How to assert yourself, listen to others, and resolve conflicts.* New York: Simon & Schuster.

Bowers, C. A., & Flinders, D. J. (1991). *Culturally responsive teaching and supervision: A handbook for staff development.* New York: Teachers College Press.

Bridges, E. M. (1986). *The incompetent teacher.* Philadelphia: Falmer.

Calderhead, J. (1987). The quality of reflection in student teachers' professional learning. *European Journal of Teacher Education, 10,* 269-278.

Calhoun, E. F. (1994). *How to use action research in the self-renewing school.* Alexandria, VA: Association for Supervision and Curriculum Development.

Cangelosi, J. S. (1991). *Evaluating classroom instruction.* New York: London.

Clark, C., & Lampert, M. (1986). The study of teacher thinking: Implications for teacher education. *Journal of Teacher Education, 37*(5), 29-31.

Clark, D. C., & Clark, S. N. (1996). Better preparation of educational leaders. *Educational Researcher, 25*(8), 18-20.

Cogan, M. L. (1973). *Clinical supervision.* Boston: Houghton Mifflin.

Cogan, M., Anderson, R. H., & Krajewski, R. (1993). *Clinical supervision: Special methods for the supervision of teachers* (3rd ed.). Fort Worth, TX: Harcourt Brace.

Colton, A. B., & Sparks-Langer, G. M. (1993). A conceptual framework to guide the development of teacher reflection and decision making. *Journal of Teacher Education, 44*(1), 45-54.

Consortium on Chicago School Research. (1996). *Charting reform in Chicago: The students speak.* Chicago: Author.

Costa, A. L., & Garmston, R. J. (1994). *Cognitive coaching: A foundation for renaissance schools.* Norwood, MA: Christopher-Gordon.

Cutler, B., Cook, P., & Young, J. (1989, February). *The empowerment of preservice teachers through reflective teaching*. Paper presented at the annual meeting of the Association of Teacher Educators, St. Louis, MO.

Darling-Hammond, L. (1996). The quiet revolution: Rethinking teacher development. *Educational Leadership, 53*(6), 4-10.

Darling-Hammond, L., & McLaughlin, M. (1995). Policies that support professional development in an era of reform. *Phi Delta Kappan, 76*(8), 597-604.

Dewey, J. (1933). *How we think.* Lexington, MA: D. C. Heath.

Dowling, G., & Sheppard, K. (1976, March). *Teacher training: A counseling focus.* Paper presented at the national convention of Teachers of English to Speakers of Other Languages, New York.

Eisner, E. (1982). An artistic approach to supervision. In T. J. Sergiovanni (Ed.), *Supervision of teaching* (pp. 53-66). Alexandria, VA: Association for Supervision and Curriculum Development.

Eltis, K., & Turney, C. (1992). *Generic competencies for beginning teachers.* Draft report for the National Project on the Quality of Teaching and Learning.

Feiman-Nemser, S. (1990). Teacher preparation: Structural and conceptual alternatives. In W. T. Houston (Ed.), *Handbook of research on teacher education* (pp. 212-233). New York: Macmillan.

Fishbein, M., & Ajzen, I. (1975). *Belief, attitude, intention, and behavior: An introduction to theory and research.* Reading, MA: Addison-Wesley.

Foster, W. (1986). *Paradigms and promises: New approaches to educational administration.* Buffalo, NY: Prometheus.

Frederiksen, N. (1984). Implications of cognitive theory for instruction in problem solving. *Review of Educational Research, 4*(3), 363-407.

Freidus, H. (1991, April). *Critical issues in the curriculum of teacher education programs.* Paper presented at the annual meeting of the American Educational Research Association, Chicago.

Freire, P. (1985). *The politics of education: Culture, power and liberation.* Hadley, MA: Bergin & Garvey.

Fullan, M., & Miles, M. (1992). Getting reform right: What works and what doesn't. *Phi Delta Kappan, 73*(10), 744-752.

Fuller, F. (1970). *Personalized education for teachers: An introduction for teacher educators* (Report No. 001). Austin: The University of Texas, Research and Development Center for Teacher Education.

Fuller, J. J., & Brown, O. H. (1975). Becoming a teacher. In K. Ryan (Ed.), *Teacher education: The 74th yearbook of the National Society for the Study of Education, Part II* (pp. 25-52). Chicago: University of Chicago Press.

Gagne, R. M. (1968). Learning hierarchies. In M. D. Merrill (Ed.), *Instructional design: Readings* (pp. 118-131). Englewood Cliffs, NJ: Prentice Hall.

Garman, N. B. (1982). The clinical approach to supervision. In T. J. Sergiovanni (Ed.), *Supervision of teaching* (pp. 35-52). Alexandria, VA: Association for Supervision and Curriculum Development.

Garman, N. B. (1990). Theories embedded in the events of clinical supervision: A hermeneutic approach. *Journal of Curriculum and Supervision, 5*(3), 201-213.

Gilson, J. (1989). *Reconstructive reflective teaching: A review of the literature.* (ERIC Document Reproduction Service No. ED 327 481)

Giroux, H. A. (1992). Educational leadership and the crisis of democratic government. *Educational Research, 21*(4), 4-11.

Gitlin, A., Ogawa, R. T., & Rose, E. (1984). Supervision, reflection, and understanding: A case for horizontal evaluation. *Journal of Teacher Education, 35,* 46-52.

Glanz, J. (1995). Exploring supervision history: An invitation and agenda. *Journal of Curriculum and Supervision, 10*(2), 95-113.

Glanz, J. (1997a). Has the field of supervision evolved to a point that it should be called something else? No. In J. Glanz & R. F. Neville (Eds.), *Educational supervision: Perspectives, issues, and controversies* (pp. 124-130). Norwood, MA: Christopher-Gordon.

Glanz, J. (1997b). Most critical issue in supervision? Response. *Instructional Supervision Newsletter, 17*(1), 6.

Glanz, J. (1997c). The Tao of supervision: Taoist insights into the theory and practice of educational supervision. *Journal of Curriculum and Supervision, 12*(3), 193-211.

Glanz, J., & Neville, R. F. (1997). *Educational supervision: Perspectives, issues, and controversies.* Norwood, MA: Christopher-Gordon.

Glaser, B. G. (1978). *Theoretical sensitivity: Advances in the methodology of grounded theory.* Mill Valley, CA: Sociology.

Glaser, B. G., & Strauss, A. L. (1967). *The discovery of grounded theory: Strategies for qualitative research.* Chicago: Aldine.

Glasner, S. E. (1997). *Preservice teachers' metacognitive and reflective thinking and teaching practices: The influence of university supervisors' and cooperating teachers' verbal guidance.* Unpublished manuscript, The University of Georgia at Athens.

Glass, G. V. (1982). Meta-analysis: An approach to the synthesis of research results. *Journal of Research in Science Teaching, 19*(2), 93-112.

Glickman, C. D. (1981). *Developmental supervision: Alternative approaches for helping teachers improve instruction.* Alexandria, VA: Association for Supervision and Curriculum Development.

Glickman, C. D. (1985). *Supervision of instruction: A developmental approach.* Boston: Allyn & Bacon.

Glickman, C. D. (1991). Pretending not to know what we know. *Educational Leadership, 48*(8), 4-10.

Glickman, C. D. (Ed.). (1992). *Supervision in transition.* Alexandria, VA: Association for Supervision and Curriculum Development.

Glickman, C. D., Gordon, S. P., & Ross-Gordon, J. M. (1995). *Supervision of instruction: A developmental approach* (3rd ed.). Boston: Allyn & Bacon.

Goldhammer, R. (1969). *Clinical supervision: Special methods for the supervision of teachers.* New York: Holt, Rinehart & Winston.

Goldsberry, L. F. (1980). *Colleague consultation: Teacher collaboration using a clinical supervision method.* Unpublished doctoral dissertation, University of Illinois, Urbana.

Gordon, S. P. (1997). Has the field of supervision evolved to a point that it should be called something else? In J. Glanz & R. F. Neville (Eds.),

Educational supervision: Perspectives, issues, and controversies (pp. 114-123). Norwood, MA: Christopher-Gordon.

Gore, J., & Zeichner, K. (1991). Action research and reflective teaching in preservice teacher education: A case study from the United States. *Teaching and Teacher Education, 7,* 119-136.

Grant, C., & Zeichner, K. (1984). On becoming a reflective teacher. In C. Grant (Ed.), *Preparing for reflective teaching* (pp. 1-18) Boston: Allyn & Bacon.

Green, J. L., & Wallat, C. (Vol. Eds.). (1981). *Ethnography and language in educational settings.* In R. O. Freedle (Ed.), *Discourse processes: Advances in research and theory: Vol. 5.* Norwood, NJ: Ablex.

Grimmett, P. P. (1984, April). *A study of the relationship of supervisor and teacher conceptual level during classroom improvement conferences.* Paper presented at the annual meeting of the American Educational Research Association, New Orleans.

Grimmett, P. P. (1988). The nature of reflection and Schön's conception in perspective. In P. P. Grimmett & G. Erickson (Eds.), *Reflection in teacher education* (pp. 5-15). New York: Teachers College Press.

Grimmett, P. P., & Crehan, E. P. (1992). The nature of collegiality in teacher development: The case of clinical supervision. In A. Hargreaves & M. Fullan (Eds.), *Teacher development and educational change* (pp. 56-85). London: Falmer.

Grimmett, P. P., & Erickson, G. (Eds.). (1988). *Reflection in teacher education.* New York: Teachers College Press.

Habermas, J. (1978) *Knowledge and human interests* (2nd English ed.; J. J. Shapiro Trans.). London: Heinemann Educational. (Original work published 1968)

Hallinger, P., & Murphy, J. (1987). Assessing and developing principal instructional leadership. *Educational Leadership, 45*(1), 54-61.

Hancock, V. (1993). *Information literacy for lifelong learning.* Syracuse, NY: ERIC Clearinghouse on Information Resources. (ERIC Document Reproduction Service No. ED 358 870)

Hargreaves, A. (1990). *Contrived collegiality: The micropolitics of teacher collaboration.* Toronto: Ontario Institute for Studies in Education.

Hatton, N., & Smith, D. (1995). Reflection in teacher education: Towards definition and implementation. *Teaching & Teacher Education, 11*(1), 33-49.

Hekelman, F., & Blase, J. R. (1996). Excellence in clinical teaching: The core of the mission. *Academic Medicine, 71*(7), 36-40.

Herbert, J. M., & Tankersley, M. (1993). More and less effective ways to intervene with classroom teachers. *Journal of Curriculum and Supervision, 9*(1), 24-40.

Hipp, K. A. (1995). *Exploring the relationship between principals' leadership behaviors and teachers' sense of efficacy in Wisconsin middle schools.* Unpublished doctoral dissertation, University of Wisconsin—Madison.

Holland, P. E. (1989). Implicit assumptions about the supervisory conference: A review and analysis of literature. *Journal of Curriculum and Supervision, 4,* 362-379.

Houston, W. (1988). Reflecting on reflection. In H. Waxman et al. (Eds.), *Images of reflection in teacher education* (pp. 2-9). Reston, VA: Association of Teacher Educators.

Hunter, M. (1979). Teaching is decision making. *Educational Leadership, 37*(1), 62-67.

Hunter, M. (1980). Six types of supervisory conferences. *Educational Leadership, 37*(5), 408-412.

Hunter, M. (1987). The Hunter model of clinical supervision. In ASCA, *A practical guide for instructional supervision: A tool for administrators and supervisors.* Curriculum and Instruction Leaders Committee, Association of California School Administrators.

Hymes, D. (1971). Sociolinguistics and the ethnography of speaking [Monograph]. In E. Ardener (Ed.), *Social Anthropology and Linguistics, 10,* 47-93.

Hymes, D. (1982). *Ethnolinguistic study of classroom discourse final report.* Washington, DC: National Institute of Education.

Joyce, B., & Calhoun, E. F. (1995). School renewal: An inquiry, not a formula. *Educational Leadership, 52*(7), 51-55.

Joyce, B. R., & Calhoun, E. F. (1996). *Creating learning experiences: The role of instructional theory and research.* Alexandria, VA: Association for Supervision and Curriculum Development.

Joyce, B., & Showers, B. (1983). *Power in staff development through research on training.* Washington, DC: Association for Supervision and Curriculum Development.

Joyce, B., & Showers, B. (1995). *Student achievement through staff development* (2nd ed.). New York: Longman.

Joyce, B., & Weil, M. (1996). *Models of teaching* (5th ed.). Boston: Allyn & Bacon.

Kraft, R. E. (1991, April). *Gender differences in the supervisory process.* Paper presented at the annual meeting of the American Educational Research Association, Chicago.

Krajewski, R. (1996). Supervision 2015. *Wingspan, 11*(2), 15-17.

Larsen, M. L., & Malen, B. (1997, April). *The elementary school principals' influence on teachers' curricular and instructional decisions.* Paper presented at the annual meeting of the American Educational Research Association, Chicago.

Leithwood, K. (1994). Leadership for school restructuring. *Educational Administration Quarterly, 30*(4), 498-518.

Lewis, L., & Dowling, L. (1992). Meaning making and reflective practice. *Adult Learning, 3*(4), 7.

Little, J. W. (1993). Teachers' professional development in a climate of educational reform. *Educational Evaluation and Policy Analysis, 15*(2), 129-151.

Lortie, D. C. (1975). *School teacher: A sociological study.* Chicago: University of Chicago Press.

Louis, K. S., Marks, H. M., & Kruse, S. (1996). Teachers' professional community in restructuring schools. *American Educational Research Journal, 33*(4), 757-789.

Loup, K. S. (1995, April). *Linking school professional learning environment characteristics, teacher self and organizational efficacies, and receptivity to change to multiple indices of school effectiveness: Implications for school administration.* Paper presented at the annual meeting of the American Educational Research Association, San Francisco.

Manning, B. H., & Payne, B. D. (1996). *Self-talk for teachers and students: Metacognitive strategies for personal and classroom use.* Boston: Allyn & Bacon.

Marchant, G. J. (1989). Metateaching: A metaphor for reflective teaching. *Education, 109*(4), 487-489.

May, W. T., & Zimpher, N. L. (1986). An examination of three theoretical perspectives on supervision: Perceptions of preservice field supervision. *Journal of Curriculum and Supervision, 1,* 83-99.

McBride, M., & Skau, K. G. (1995). Trust, empowerment, and reflection: Essentials of supervision. *Journal of Curriculum and supervision, 10*(3), 262-277.

McGregor, D. (1960). *The human side of enterprise.* New York: McGraw-Hall.

Mead, G. H. (1934). *Mind, self, and society.* Chicago: University of Chicago Press.

Meier, D. (1995). *The power of their ideas.* Boston: Beacon.

Meyer, S. (1992). Cultivating reflection-in-action in trainer development. *Adult Learning, 3*(4), 16-17, 31.

Miles, M. B., & Huberman, A. M. (1984). *Qualitative data analysis: A source book of new methods.* Beverly Hills, CA: Sage.

Mosher, R. L., & Purpel, D. E. (1972). *Supervision: The reluctant profession.* Boston: Houghton Mifflin.

Murphy, J. (1995). Rethinking the foundations of leadership preparation: Insights from school improvement efforts. *Design for Leadership: The Bulletin of the National Policy Board for Educational Administration, 6*(1), 1-4, 6.

Noddings, N. (1986). Fidelity in teaching, teacher education, and research for teaching. *Harvard Educational Review, 56*(4), 496-510.

Nolan, J. F. (1989). Can supervisory practice embrace Schön's view of reflective supervision? *Journal of Curriculum and Supervision, 4*(1), 35-40.

Osterman, K. F. (1990). Reflective practice: A new agenda for education. *Education and Urban Society, 22*(2), 134.

Osterman, K. F., & Kottkamp, R. B. (1993). *Reflective practice for educators: Improving schooling through professional development.* Newbury Park, CA: Corwin.

Ovando, M. N. (1991). Delivering clinical supervision based on the formative dimension of the Texas Teacher Appraisal System. *Wingspan: Pedamorphosis Communique, 7*(1), 21-29.

Pajak, E. (1989). *Identification of supervisory proficiencies project* (Final report, University of Georgia). Alexandria, VA: Association for Supervision and Curriculum Development.

Pajak, E. (1993). *Approaches to clinical supervision: Alternatives for improving instruction.* Norwood, MA: Christopher-Gordon.

Pajak, E., & Glickman, C. (1989). Informational and controlling language in simulated supervisory conferences. *American Educational Research Journal, 26*(1), 93-106.

Pasch, M. T., Arpin, D., Kragt, J., Garcia, J., & Harberts, M. (1990). *Evaluation of teachers' instructional decision making.* Paper presented at the annual meeting of the Michigan Educational Research Association, Novi, Michigan.

Phillips, M. D., & Glickman, C. D. (1991). Peer coaching: Developmental approach to enhance teacher thinking. *Journal of Staff Development, 12*(2), 20-25.

Prawat, R. S. (1991). Conversations with self and settings: A framework for thinking about teacher empowerment. *American Educational Research Journal, 28*(4), 737-757.

Prawat, R. S. (1993). The role of the principal in the development of learning communities. *Wingspan, 9*(2), 7-9.

Pugach, M. (1990, April). *Self study: The genesis of reflection in novice teachers.* Paper presented at the annual meeting of the American Educational Research Association, Boston.

Pugach, M. C., & Johnson, L. J. (1990). Fostering the continued democratization of consultation through action research. *Teacher Education and Special Education, 13*(3-4), 240-245.

Raywid, M. (1993). Finding time for collaboration. *Educational Leadership, 51*(1), 30-34.

Reitzug, U. C. (1994). A case study of empowering principal behavior. *American Educational Research Journal, 31*(2), 283-307.

Reitzug, U. C., & Cross, B. (1993, October). *Deconstructing principal instructional leadership: From "super" vision to critical collaboration.* Paper presented at the annual conference of the University Council for Educational Administration, Houston, TX.

Retallick, J. A. (1990, April). *Clinical supervision and the structure of communication.* Paper presented at the annual meeting of the American Educational Research Association, Boston.

Roberts, J. (1988). Training for effective instructional supervision: Using the research. *NASSP Bulletin, 72*(511), 73-77.

Roberts, J. (1989a). Expert supervisory practice: Integrating expert pedagogy and reflective practice. *ASCD Instructional Supervision Network Newsletter, 2*(3), 3-4.

Roberts, J. (1989b). Re-energizing teaching through the evolution of peer coaching: Moving from direct supervision to collegial reflection and passion in teaching. *ASCD Instructional Supervision Network Newsletter, 3*(2), 1-2.

Roberts, J. (1989c). A study of aspiring administrators' problems in conducting instructional conferences. *AASA Professor, 11*(3), 5-8.

Roberts, J. (1991a). Administrator training: The instructional conference component. *Journal of Educational Administration, 29*(2), 38-49.

Roberts, J. (1991b). In preparation for the principalship: Initiates' problems in conducting instructional conferences. *Journal of Educational Administration, 29*(2), 38-49.

Roberts, J. (1992a). Face-threatening acts and politeness theory: Contrasting speeches from supervisory conferences. *Journal of Curriculum and Supervision, 7*(3), 287-301.

Roberts, J. (1992b, April). *The relationship of power and involvement to experience in supervisory conference: Discourse analysis of supervisor style.* Paper presented at the annual meeting of the American Educational Research Association, San Francisco.

Roberts, J. (1994). Discourse analysis of supervisory conferences: An exploration. *Journal of Curriculum and Supervision, 9*(2), 136-154.

Ross, E. W., & Hannay, L. M. (1986). Towards a critical theory of reflective inquiry. *Journal of Teacher Education, 37,* 9-14.

Rusch, E. A. (1993, April). *Resistance to change: Fact or stereotype.* Paper presented at the annual meeting of the American Educational Research Association, Atlanta.

Schlecty, P. C. (1997). *Inventing better schools.* San Francisco: Jossey-Bass.

Schmuck, R., & Runkel, P. (1994). *Handbook of organization development in schools* (4th ed.). Prospect Heights, IL: Waveland.

Schön, D. (1983). *The reflective practitioner.* New York: Basic Books.

Schön, D. A. (1987). *Educating the reflective practitioner: Toward a new design for teaching and learning in the professions.* San Francisco: Jossey-Bass.

Schön, D. A. (1988). Coaching reflective teaching. In P. P. Grimmett & G. F. Erickson (Eds.), *Reflection in teacher education* (pp. 19-30). New York: Teachers College Press.

Sergiovanni, T. J. (1992). Moral authority and the regeneration of supervision. In C. D. Glickman (Ed.), *Supervision in transition: The 1992 ASCD Yearbook* (pp. 203-214). Reston, VA: Association for Supervision and Curriculum Development.

Sergiovanni, T. J. (1995). *The principalship: A reflective practice perspective.* Boston: Allyn & Bacon.

Sergiovanni, T. J. (1996). *Moral leadership.* San Francisco: Jossey-Bass.

Sergiovanni, T. J. (1997). How can we move toward a community theory of supervision? In J. Glanz & R. F. Neville (Eds.), *Educational supervision: Perspectives, issues, and controversies* (pp. 264-280). Norwood, MA: Christopher-Gordon.

Sergiovanni, T. J., & Starratt, R. J. (1993). *Supervision: A redefinition* (5th ed.). New York: McGraw-Hill.

Sheppard, B. (1996). Exploring the transformational nature of instructional leadership. *The Alberta Journal of Educational Research, 42*(4), 325-344.

Short, E. C. (1995). A review of studies in the first 10 volumes of the *Journal of Curriculum and Supervision. Journal of Curriculum and Supervision, 11*(1), 87-105.

Short, P. M., & Rinehart, J. S. (1992). School participant empowerment scale: Assessment of the level of empowerment within the school environment. *Educational and Psychological Measurement, 52,* 951-960.

Short, P. M., & Rinehart, J. S. (1993). Reflection as a means of developing expertise. *Educational Administration Quarterly, 29*(4), 501-521.

Showers, B., & Joyce, B. (1996). The evolution of peer coaching. *Educational Leadership, 53*(6), 12-16.

Smith, D., & Hatton, N. (1993). Reflection in teacher education: A study in progress. *Education Research and Perspectives, 20,* 13-23.

Smith, W., & Andrews, R. (1989). *Instructional leadership: How principals make a difference.* Alexandria, VA: Association for Supervision and Curriculum Development.

Smyth, J. (1985). Developing a critical practice of clinical supervision. *Journal of Curriculum Studies, 17,* 1-15.

Smyth, J. (1988). A critical perspective for clinical supervision. *Journal of Curriculum and Supervision, 3,* 136-156.

Smyth, J. (1989). Developing and sustaining critical reflection in teacher education. *Journal of Teacher Education, 40*(2), 2-9.

Smyth, J. (1990, April). *Problematizing teaching through a "critical" approach to clinical supervision.* Paper presented at the annual conference of the American Educational Research Association, Boston.

Smyth, J. (1997). Is supervision more than the surveillance of instruction? In J. Glanz & R. F. Neville (Eds.), *Educational supervision: Perspectives, issues, and controversies* (pp. 286-295). Norwood, MA: Christopher-Gordon.

Soder, R. (Ed.). (1995). *Democracy, education, and the schools.* San Francisco: Jossey-Bass.

Sparks-Langer, G. M., & Colton, A. B. (1991). Synthesis of research on teachers' reflective thinking. *Education Leadership, 48*(6), 37-44.

Sparks-Langer, G. M., Simmons, J. M., Pasch, M., Colton, A., & Starko, A. (1990). Reflective pedagogical thinking: How can we promote it and measure it? *Journal of Teacher Education, 41*(4), 23-32.

Sprinthall, N. A., Reiman, A. J., & Thies-Sprinthall, L. (1996). Teacher professional development. In J. Sikula, T. J. Buttery, & E. Guyton (Eds.), *Handbook of research on teacher education* (2nd ed., pp. 666-703). New York: Macmillan.

St. Maurice, H. (1987). Clinical supervision and power: Regimes of instructional management. In T. S. Popkewitz (Ed.), *Critical studies in teacher education: Its folklore, theory and practice* (pp. 242-264). New York: Falmer.

Valli, L. (1992). *Reflective teacher education: Cases and critiques.* Albany: State University of New York Press.

van Manen, M. J. (1977). Linking ways of knowing with ways of being practical. *Curriculum Inquiry, 6*(3), 205-228.

van Mannen, M. (1991). *The tact of teaching: The meaning of pedagogical thoughtfulness.* Albany: State University of New York Press.

Villars, J. (1991). *Restructuring through school redesign.* Bloomington, IN: Phi Delta Kappa.

Vygotsky, L. S. (1978). *Mind in society: The development of higher psychological processes.* Cambridge, MA: Harvard University Press. (Original work published 1930, 1933, 1935)

Waite, D. (1992). Supervisors' talk: Making sense of conferences from an anthropological linguistic perspective. *Journal of Curriculum and Supervision, 7*(4), 349-371.

Waite, D. (1995). *Rethinking instructional supervision: Notes on its language and culture.* London: Falmer.

Waxman, H. C., & Walberg, H. J. (Eds.). (1991). *Effective teaching: Current research.* Berkeley, CA: McCutchan.

Wolf, J. (1994). *BLT: A resource handbook for building leadership teams.* Minneapolis, MN: The North Central Association of Schools and Colleges.

Zeichner, K. M., & Liston, D. (1985). Varieties of discourse in supervisory conferences. *Teaching and Teacher Education, 1,* 155-174.

Zeichner, K. M., & Liston, D. P. (1987). Teaching student teachers to reflect. *Harvard Educational Review, 57*(1), 23-48.

Zepeda, S. J., Wood, F. H., & O'Hair, M. J. (1996). A vision of supervision for 21st century schooling: Trends to promote change, inquiry, and reflection. *Wingspan, 11*(2), 26-30.

Zimpher, N. L., deVoss, G. G., & Nott, D. L. (1980). A closer look at university student teacher supervision. *Journal of Teacher Education, 31*, 11-15.

Index

CORWIN
PRESS

The Corwin Press logo—a raven striding across an open book—represents the happy union of courage and learning. We are a professional-level publisher of books and journals for K-12 educators, and we are committed to creating and providing resources that embody these qualities. Corwin's motto is "Success for All Learners."